Mirei Shigemori
MODERNIZING THE JAPANESE GARDEN

Mirei Shigemori
MODERNIZING THE JAPANESE GARDEN

Christian Tschumi

Photographs by
Markuz Wernli Saitō

Stone Bridge Press
Berkeley, California

FRONT COVER
Courtyard with characteristic stone waves at Fukuchi-in

BACK COVER
"Garden in the Color of Love" at Fukuchi-in

FRONT FLAP
**"Mirei"; Shigemori's adopted first name was inspired by the
name of the famous French landscape painter Jean-François
Millet (1814–75)**

BACK FLAP
Niwa, **meaning "garden"**

Published by
Stone Bridge Press
P.O. Box 8208, Berkeley, CA 94707 • tel 510-524-8732 • sbp@stonebridge.com • www.stonebridge.com

For comments regarding the content of this book, contact the author at ctschumi@post.harvard.edu.

This work was made possible by generous grants from
The Graham Foundation for Advanced Studies in the Fine Arts and from the Nisshō Iwai Foundation.

By convention, Japanese proper names appear in Western order,
that is, family name last, except for names of historical figures.

Text © 2005 Christian Tschumi.

Photographs and Illustrations © 2005 Markuz Wernli Saitō.
Book design, illustrations, and layout by Markuz Wernli Saitō.
www.markuz.com

Calligraphy on front and back flaps by Mirei Shigemori; used by permission of the Shigemori Family.
Photograph on p. 14 used by permission of Haruzō Ōhashi.

Printed in Singapore.
2005 2006 2007 2008 2009
1 2 3 4 5 6 7 8 9 10

ISBN 1-880656-94-9

3 4015 06897 6388

For Nao,
without whose infinite support
this book would not exist

Contents

Wave and sand bank framed by bamboo fence at Tenrai-an

Introduction

The book you are holding in your hands is not just another general introduction to the art of the Japanese garden. There are numerous such books available, and these accomplish the task of introducing the Japanese garden very well. They have made Kyōto gardens like the ones at Ginkaku-ji, the Katsura Imperial Villa, and Ryōan-ji world famous.

This smaller volume instead focuses on a single aspect of the Japanese garden and, more than that, on a particular person's work. Here we are interested in the contemporary renewal of an older garden type called *karesansui*, the dry landscape garden. In the West the *karesansui* is often referred to as a Zen garden; its most prominent representative is at the above-mentioned Ryōan-ji and was most likely made in the Muromachi period (1333–1568).

"We cannot say that people are really living if they are not also living with nature, that is, living within the garden. Gardens play an important role in our health, just as in olden times there was the saying 'In houses where gardeners come and go, there is no need for the doctor.' The garden is essential to our life and not something we can do without." [1]

Most of Japan's well-known gardens are at least several hundred years old, products of a time long past. Perhaps you are wondering what Japanese gardens look like these days. The picture is very mixed. There are many garden makers who seem to care little about the old traditions and get most of their inspiration from contemporary Western designs. Then there is a small

Landscape of a protected inland bay at Zuihō-in

group of gardeners who try to understand their roots and who base their work upon the long history that garden art has in Japan. Among this second group is where the subject of this book, Mirei Shigemori, can be found. After looking through the following pages you may agree with us that Shigemori's approach to the renewal of the Japanese garden is well worth considering when building new gardens these days.

Renewal here is, as Mirei Shigemori understood it, the continuous development of the art of the Japanese garden. A project begun long ago was to be continued into the future, otherwise the art would no longer be alive. According to Shigemori, those earlier times when highly educated Japanese aristocrats engaged in garden making saw the creation of many gardens of high quality. Later, when the professional garden makers took over, creativity was replaced by the nostalgic copying of existing famous garden designs or well-known landscapes. This tendency was further strengthened by the appearance of the first garden-making manuals in the Edo period (1603–1868); these popularized the art

The Red Phoenix stone setting at Sekizō-ji

and were, again according to Shigemori, one of the main reasons for the widespread mediocrity and stagnation in garden making.

The dictionary says that "to renew" means "to restore to freshness, vigor, or perfection" and it is that sense of the word that applies to Mirei Shigemori's efforts. He introduced new materials like concrete and used them in completely new ways. He formed winding lines that depicted waves or clouds. He also brought in color that he mixed into the concrete or used to produce different colors of gravel for the garden's surfaces. It is both these new shapes and their colors that make Shigemori's gardens modern, at least when compared to their Japanese predecessors. But by also incorporating past traditions and elements, Shigemori remained close to the roots of his trade. He, like gardeners of old, continued to set stones, but he slightly twisted the technique and its related references. He kept using sand, but introduced new colors and raked the planes in different and fresh patterns. Hence in Shigemori's gardens the modern element works so successfully because it remains in a traditional context, without obscuring the past tradition.

Shigemori was fascinated by his own culture. He didn't think much of ideas that were just copied from the past or imported from another culture. For him the essence of the Japanese garden, and the culture that surrounded it, was strong, rich, and alive. In the art of tea as well as in *ikebana* he saw a cultural heritage that needed to be explored and learned from. He regarded the Japanese garden as a unique cultural achievement of the highest order. Although the art had come to lack creative energy, he was ready to write the next chapter in its development. Shigemori had a vision of how to develop—and hence preserve—the art of the Japanese garden.

How This Book Came About

Many people are attracted by the Japanese garden, and so was the author of this book, a gardener by heart and education. By my early twenties I had already worked for half a year with a landscape gardener in Ōsaka. Ever since I had wanted to return to these islands, but held off until April 2000, when a scholarship sponsored by the Japanese Ministry of Education allowed me to move to Japan and start my research on the renewal of the Japanese garden. My work eventually developed into a four-year research project and a substantial dissertation. This book draws on that experience.

Before leaving for Japan I had met a fellow Swiss, visual artist and photographer Markuz Wernli. Markuz's new and surprising look at the Japanese garden through his cameras fascinated me. Over the course of two years Markuz took close to 1,500 images of some of Mirei Shigemori's most interesting gardens. With the support of Stone Bridge Press, Markuz and I are now able to present you with this fresh look at the Japanese garden.

Organization

This book features a selection of ten of the most interesting gardens designed by Mirei Shigemori. By "interesting" I mean those works that have made a great or unusual contribution to the renewal of the Japanese garden. In its own way each of the gardens profiled here provides a look at how the dry landscape garden can be renewed and

---

LEGEND FOR GARDEN ILLUSTRATIONS

	Stone setting
	Moss
	Vegetation (tree, shrub)
	Gravel
	Building foundation, platform
	Covered walkway
	Closed building
	Stone path, stepping stone
	Water, pond, moat
	Wall (clay, stone, concrete)
	Fence, gate (wood, bamboo)
	Metal gate
	Stone lantern
①②③④	**Plan references**

---

maybe even a glimpse into the direction this garden type will evolve in the future.

The ten gardens are presented in chronological order, beginning with Mirei Shigemori's early masterpiece, the garden at Tōfuku-ji built in 1939, and continuing all the way to his very last work at Matsuo Taisha that features possibly the best stone setting he ever made. Along the way we document the milestones of Shigemori's career—his first use of the element of line as well as his introduction of different colors of gravel—and in so doing present the materials with which he modernized the Japanese garden.

The timeline at the end of the book will help the reader understand the sequence of gardens in conjunction with important events in Mirei Shigemori's life.

Markuz's photographs are of course a world of their own. They accompany the chapters describing the gardens, and in most cases you will find in them the elements mentioned in the text. But as these elements are sometimes shown in close-up and at other times in the distance, getting a sense

On the borderline of tsukiyama and the sea at Tōfuku-ji

of the whole garden may take a bit of imagination. While attracting you to the gardens, these images should still leave enough unrevealed so that if you ever visit them in person you will have many more things to discover. The book is not a garden guide per se, but for those readers who are interested in seeing the gardens themselves we provide address information in the back, together with some maps.

Additional information about some of the points raised in the text are in the Notes. Japanese words that are used frequently but that are likely unfamiliar to nonspecialist readers appear in a separate Glossary for easy reference.

Who Was Mirei Shigemori?

The Kyōto scholar and landscape architect Mirei Shigemori (1896–1975) made the evolution of the Japanese garden his life's objective. Hardly known in the West, he is also just starting to be rediscovered in his home country of Japan. Largely because of his quite radical approach he remains a controversial person in the field of the Japanese gar-

Mirei Shigemori, around 1970

den. But considering his contributions to the renewal of garden culture in Japan, both in written and built form, Shigemori's outsider status is sure to change in the near future.

Born in 1896 in the village of Yoshikawa in the countryside near Okayama City, 180 km west of Kyōto, Mirei Shigemori started to study the tea ceremony and *ikebana* (flower arranging) when he was a teenager. In 1917, at the age of twenty-one, he went to Tōkyō to study *nihonga* (Japanese painting), art history, and philosophy. After his graduation from the Tōkyō Fine Arts School he stayed in Tōkyō to work on the establishment of a University of Culture (Bunka Daigakuin). But this project came to a halt when on 1 September 1923 the Great Kantō Earthquake struck. As a result Shigemori moved back to his hometown of Yoshikawa, where he worked as a part-time farmer and scholar while teaching a philosophy class in town. In 1929 he moved to Kyōto, where he would remain for the rest of his life. He became very active in the field of *ikebana*, and between 1930 and 1932 he worked on his first major publication, the nine-volume *Complete Works of Japanese Flower Arrangement Art,* which was published in Kyōto.[2] In 1932 Shigemori was asked to write the *Garden* edition for the twelve-volume Art in Kyōto series. For this, his first important book on the Japanese garden, Shigemori visited about a hundred gardens all around Kyōto. The results of his efforts were published in 1933 as *Art in Kyōto: Garden Edition.*[3] Not only did this book occasion Shigemori's first forays into serious garden research, it was the beginning of what would later become a much bigger project.

During this same period Shigemori took on a few early garden projects in Kyōto and Ōsaka. At first most of them were residential gardens, but in 1934 he was commissioned to design the garden at Nara's famous Kasuga Taisha shrine. This job represents Shigemori's first real commercial garden project and can thus be seen as marking the start of his career as a landscape architect.

Following his detour into the field of *ikebana* and now paralleling his new vocation as a garden maker, Shigemori undertook an extensive survey of nearly 250 gardens all over Japan. For more than three years, from 1936 to 1939, Shigemori and a small group of dedicated helpers surveyed all the gardens, took pictures, made sketches, and checked documentary records. This first-ever comprehensive survey of Japanese gardens culminated in the publication of a twenty-six-volume encyclopedia titled *Illustrated Book on the History of the Japanese Garden.*[4] This work is a unique snapshot in time, a time capsule so to speak, and still one of the greatest resources available for the study of the Japanese garden. For

Mirei Shigemori himself it was probably the best way to learn about gardens; it clearly became the most important foundation of his future work and an immeasurable source of inspiration.

"Historically speaking, Japan's past was very good, but Japan's present largely comes up empty. In 100 years, in 1,000 years, they will be wondering what people in the Meiji, Taishō, and Shōwa periods were up to. That's how dull these times are! That's why I thought I had to at least leave something good behind, so I switched to being a maker of things. Whether I was any good or not will be judged by the future, I guess." [5]

As a passionate advocate for the renewal of the Japanese garden Mirei Shigemori felt that innovation had come to a halt around the middle of the Edo period and that gardeners since then were just repeating what had been done before. Shigemori thus came to the conclusion that the job of renewing Japanese garden culture was up to him. The garden he built around Tōfuku-ji's main hall in 1939 (see pages 24–33) was his first large garden project and quite controversial at the time, although by now its image of stones scattered in a field of moss has become a symbol of the contemporary Japanese garden that is recognized around the world.

During the years of World War II Shigemori was very busy researching and writing books. Between 1940 and 1949 he published a total of thirty-three works, eight of them just in 1949, his most productive year as an author. Between 1950 and his death in 1975 Shigemori switched his emphasis to actually designing and building gardens, although in the last ten years of his life he did turn somewhat to writing again. It is in this final decade of his life that we see the creation of his most radical garden designs, many of them the ones featured in this book.

Shigemori would often do a design proposal in the form of an idea-sketch or even a full-scale plan. This he then presented to the client before the start of construction. In the early years he often was present for much of the construction, although he was not very hands-on and mainly directed the

Wave washing up to shore at Sumiyoshi Jinja

work. But the more famous he became the less he was on the site, as he became increasingly busy. It eventually came to the point where his experienced construction team would do most of the work, following the design drawings, and Shigemori would stop by only for important events like setting stones or the placement of major trees. And when he came he would always make *matcha* (whipped green tea) for everybody on the site, including his clients. He was an artist and a scholar, and he rarely put his hands on a shovel.

Waves and a 7-5-3 stone setting at Sumiyoshi Jinja

Mirei Shigemori died at the age of seventy-nine, shortly after having finished the amazing stone setting at Matsuo Taisha (see pages 106–15).

Mirei Shigemori's Garden Art

The type of garden most often built by Mirei Shigemori is what the Japanese call a *karesansui*, or dry landscape garden. In the West it is sometimes referred to as a Zen garden, but not all Zen temples have a dry landscape garden, and not all such gardens necessarily have any relationship to the Zen school of Buddhism. Shigemori in fact made several *karesansui* gardens at Shintō shrines! So in this book I will refrain from using the somewhat misleading term Zen garden and will instead refer to this garden type by the original Japanese term *karesansui*.

A *karesansui* garden is by definition dry and uses no real water. The presence of water is instead implied by larger or smaller areas of sand or gravel (usually taken from the river Shirakawa in eastern Kyōto). Rocks placed within the sand, or in a nearby area, usually signify mountains or islands in the sea. Sand, gravel, and stones thus constitute the basic and necessary palette of materials in a dry landscape garden. Plantings are not a must but are still sometimes found in this garden type. Even the most minimal or abstract *karesansui* garden might have a little moss around its stones and a plum or cherry tree near the fringe. Some of the more distinctive examples of this garden type are combined with a *karikomi*, or sculpted hedge, usually in the form of evergreen shrubs shaped by formal trimming at least twice yearly.

The Meaning of Shigemori's Gardens

The garden as an artistic creation is a reflection of its time as well as its place. At least this is how it used to be for much of the Japanese garden's history. Consequently, anyone considering the problem of its creative renewal within a specific cultural context must examine many different historical and aesthetic parameters. Mirei Shigemori was a person who knew his own culture very well, as a look at his personal history will immediately prove. He was at the same time a dedicated *ikebana* artist and a connoisseur of the tea ceremony

and its related arts. Indeed, he loved Japan and its culture so much that he never even went abroad.

But what motivated Shigemori to approach the garden as he did? Loraine Kuck suggests in her book *The World of the Japanese Garden* that "his historical studies had made clear how vitality had drained from the Japanese garden art after the middle of the Edo period when the professional garden men took over. . . . It was then that he decided to follow the earlier artist-masters and go into the creating of gardens as a serious art expression." As a consequence, Shigemori developed an approach to the modernization of the Japanese garden that was very much informed by his background as a painter. And this is at least part of the reason his works are both interesting and unique.

In a late essay titled "Shinsakuteiki" Shigemori also argues that "one can make gardens according to the ancient meanings or according to the ancient forms, but in actuality the person who is designing the garden and building it is from nowhere other than the present day. The fact that we are people who live in the present means that we are unable to make gardens that carry the meanings of olden times or have the forms of those times. If we try, we can only make a garden that is an imitation, and this is meaningless."[6] Shigemori's explorations into the roots of the Japanese garden are in fact very enlightening. He traced the Japanese garden back to the worshiping of gods who came to visit special places in the landscape, usually rock outcroppings or very old trees. It is this recognition of the garden's religious roots in combination with the consciousness of his own place in history that formed the basis for Shigemori's approach to the renewal of Japanese garden culture. At the same time he was very much aware that he lived in the present, and for him the present had to be different from the past.

Origins of the Strategy for Renewal

Both Mirei Shigemori's education in painting and his experience producing a countrywide garden survey greatly influenced his approach to the renewal of the Japanese garden. His survey work taught him about the history and development of the garden, while his training as a painter was largely responsible for the approach he took in his own garden creations.

Being a garden maker with a painter's eyes, Shigemori loved the abstractness of the *karesansui* garden and realized what enormous potential this garden type had for the future of Japanese garden culture. Throughout his career he persistently explored options for the modernization of the garden

Color and a geometric element: red concrete at Fukuchi-in (LEFT) and lines of stone at Kishiwada-jō (RIGHT)

through adaptations in form and material. But while doing this he always remained close to the original prototype, knowing that "the artistic value of the garden is proportionate to the degree of simplification carried out."[7] Looking at his work we do have to say that Shigemori's most artistic gardens are usually rather simple and surprise the viewer with a new element being added to an otherwise largely unchanged context. At the same time the designer understood the value of empty spaces. In the same book Shigemori notes, "These places, because of the very fact that they are vacant, stimulate one's imagination. In this respect, these areas can be called the ones left open for observers to create their own scenery." This is a lesson he might have already learned in his earlier years studying painting.

Shigemori's painterly training becomes especially evident if we take a look at the design elements he used in his *karesansui* gardens. His major adaptations to the genre can be seen in two categories: geometric elements and color. To the points of stone and the plane of gravel, Shigemori added the line as an independent element. And the plane of gravel was no longer restricted to a single color, but could appear in up to four different colors. Both of these important adaptations are illustrated by several of the gardens in this book.

The Significance of Shigemori's Work

Shigemori's trademark shape: a series of colorful waves of stone at Fukuchi-in

The sheer amount of written and built work Shigemori contributed during the seventy-nine years of his life makes him one of the most important figures in the evolution of the modern Japanese garden. He built more than 240 gardens, most of them in the Kansai (south-central Honshū) area, and in more than eighty books he wrote down his thoughts on the tea ceremony, *ikebana*, and of course the garden. Moreover, no one in the twentieth century proposed adaptations to the Japanese garden that were more radical. Inspired by his background as a painter, Shigemori often experimented with geometric forms and areas of color, hence opening up a new perspective on the continuous development of the Japanese garden. The results feel contemporary and are without a doubt visually very attractive.

Shigemori's body of work is a compelling manifesto for continuous cultural renewal. He was a person who believed that once an art form became stuck in the past and stopped developing, it was dead. His studies in art history and his survey of hundreds of gardens all over Japan made it clear to him that the garden as an artistic achievement was trapped under its own heavy load of history and needed to be freed. So he set out to continue what he had started earlier in the discipline of *ike-*

bana: to renew the cultural heritage of the art and transfer it into the present times. Hence his chief contribution was to identify possibilities for the modernization of the Japanese garden. And thanks to his amazing productivity, we now have a large body of works that explore these possibilities in material form. The following pages provide you with a first selection of Mirei Shigemori's garden art.

I would like to acknowledge the great support we received from the many garden owners, who were all very welcoming, opening up their gardens for us to take pictures and answering our many questions with great sincerity. And of course without Markuz's inspiring photographs this book would simply not be what it is. Furthermore I want to thank Peter Goodman for so carefully editing my manuscript and again Markuz Wernli Saitō, who was also responsible for the book's layout and its cover design.

Tōfuku-ji, 1939

The gardens at Tōfuku-ji's main hall are an early masterpiece among Mirei Shigemori's works and are now considered the epitome of the contemporary Japanese garden. The arrangement of square stones among thick green moss has achieved iconic status and inspired numerous garden makers throughout the world.

HISTORY Tōfuku-ji is the head temple of the Tōfuku-ji sect of the Rinzai school of Zen Buddhism. Kujō Michiie, grandson of the chief adviser to Emperor Kujō Kanezane, is said to have founded the temple on 21 July 1239. The temple's name was derived from the names of two nearby temples in what is now Nara Prefecture: *Tō* is taken from Tōdai-ji and *fuku* is from Kōfuku-ji. Apparently the Kujō clan sold their house and all their property in order to build this temple!

On 23 August 1938, head priest Sonoisan Saidō contacted Mirei Shigemori and asked him to prepare a master plan for the improvement of the general scenery at Tōfuku-ji over the next one hundred years.[8] Shigemori started immediately by surveying the entire Tōfuku-ji temple complex. The surroundings of the *hōjō* (main hall) were particularly unsightly, so eventually the priest asked Shigemori for a garden design that would improve conditions there. Shigemori noted the details of this conversation as follows:

South garden; westward view from corridor ❶ to ❺

PRIEST: "It is good for the spiritual richness of a temple when it doesn't have enough money. But it is time for me as head priest to think about having a garden here at the main hall."

SHIGEMORI: "There is no better place for a garden than the area around the *hōjō*. If I were to make a garden here, my work would live forever at this temple. I would even pay to be asked to do a project here or simply donate a garden design."

PRIEST: "I appreciate that very much, and you shall be the one I ask. So please accept our request to make a garden here, and we in return will regularly pray for your soul, now and forever.[9] And we shall not interfere with your work at all, so you may do whatever you deem appropriate."

SHIGEMORI: "All right, I will put all my energy into creating a garden here. But I will not accept any requests for changes."

PRIEST: "In that case, before you start, I have one thing I need to tell you. In our Zen sect, nothing is allowed to go to waste. So I would like to ask you, if possible, to reuse the paving stones piled up over there at the gate."

South garden with Hōjō, Hōrai, and Eijū stone settings ① to ③

SHIGEMORI: "I am already aware of that and shall include those in my proposal. To include discarded materials is always part of my garden making, but I would like to ask you to leave how to reuse them up to me."

PRIEST: "There is no need for further explanation. Today is a great day for Tōfuku-ji."[10]

Shigemori was at that time not yet famous and at least as poor as the temple. But he realized what a great opportunity it was to make a garden at such a noted place and therefore decided to work for free. No doubt he was also attracted by the promise of freedom with regard to design. Construction of the Tōfuku-ji garden started on 27 June 1939, and everything was finished by 11 November of the same year.

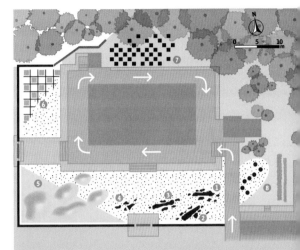

FULL NAME
Tōfuku-ji Hōjō Teien, Hassō no Niwa (The Garden of Eight Views).

LOCATION ❶ 🗾
Higashiyama-ku in Kyōto; 1.5 km southwest of Kyōto Station.

CATEGORY
A contemporary temple garden in *karesansui* style.

THEME
Views of eight mythical landscapes arranged around the four sides of the *hōjō*, the temple's main hall.

WHEN TO VISIT
The garden is open to the general public and can be visited year round. The small gorge to the north of the main hall is famous for its fall color, so visitors in autumn will be sharing the space with busloads of other tourists. In the summer months of July and August the moss in the south part of the garden is often more brown than green. On a January afternoon you might have the garden all to yourself.

DESCRIPTION The gardens at Tōfuku-ji's main hall consist of four more or less independent parts. As you approach the *hōjō*, the first garden to appear on the left is the south garden. There are four stone settings representing the islands of the immortals and further west five moss-covered mounds, symbolizing the five Zen sects of Kyōto. From east to west the stone settings symbolize the islands Hōjō ❶, Hōrai ❷, and Eijū ❸, and the group immediately west of the gate represents the Koryō islands ❹.[11] A straight diagonal line from the northwest corner of the garden to the gate divides the area of moss from the white sand and makes for a quite modern accent in the garden's layout. Two of the mounds ❺ extend into the sea, and one is an island completely surrounded by the ocean of sand.

Continue clockwise around the building and you arrive at the west garden ❻, featuring a layout inspired by the look of rice fields in a landscape. The design is simple: recycled stone curbs describe a checkerboard grid pattern filled with white sand and shaped azaleas for contrast in color, texture, and three-dimensional variation. These days, moss also covers most of the southern half of this part of the garden.

Just around the corner, to the north of the *hōjō*, you will then find the famed grid of stone plates sitting in the moss ❼. A semicircular space with azaleas and maples on its fringe, the grid starts in the southwest corner and fades out toward the northeast. It is small and enclosed with fresh green moss, the perfect contrast to the wide and dry south garden. As he promised the priest, Mirei Shigemori is here reusing the square stones of the former entrance path. The minimal design harmonizes exceptionally well with the varied backdrop.

On the way back to the entrance, you pass the east garden ❽,

LEFT **West garden; inspired by rice fields** ❻   RIGHT **North garden; seventh of eight views** ❼

situated to the east of the covered corridor. Separated from the main garden by this elevated walkway, it features a Big Dipper stone arrangement, reusing the foundation stones of the former toilet building. The constellation design is appropriately set in a cloud-shaped area of white sand.

Mirei Shigemori named the entire garden Hassō no Niwa, meaning Garden of Eight Views, a reference to the eight views he had created around the *hōjō*. The four stone settings (Hōjō, Hōrai, Eijū, and Koryō) count for a view each, and the five mounds (*gozan*) count as one, as do the grid of the north garden (*ichimatsu*), the rice fields (*seiden*), and the Big Dipper (*hokuto shichisei*). Most people seem to walk around in clockwise fashion

and thus will experience the garden in the order described here.

"A garden should have a timeless modernity; what is singularly modern in our time has no real value. A garden that can be admired by anybody at any period in time is what I think of as eternally modern." [12]

INTERPRETATION His first major contemporary garden design, the Hassō no Niwa at Tōfuku-ji expressed Mirei Shigemori's stated intention to create a modern Japanese garden—a goal he was to pursue for the rest of his life. In this early work,

LEFT **Big Dipper stone arrangement in east garden**   RIGHT **East garden stone detail**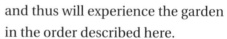

the points of the grid fading toward the east are a modern artistic expression and have no parallel among ancient Japanese gardens. Shigemori himself notes: "The technique I used made it a contemporary garden, and my main goal was timeless modernity."[13] He had first seen this grid pattern on the sliding doors of Kyōto's Katsura Rikyū and in the teahouses of Shugakuin Rikyū, both famous garden and

building complexes built in the seventeenth century.[14] The fact that this formal language now reappeared in the buildings and paintings of Modernism confirmed its timelessness and seemed to qualify the motif as eternally modern.

At Tōfuku-ji Shigemori experiments with several dot- or pointlike elements, scaling them and simplifying their form. Incorporated thematically into the designs, these elements speckle the garden's various planes; in fact, some of them look more like marks of ink on a canvas than elements of an actual garden.[15] In few if any of Shigemori's later works is the pointlike element as obvious and at the same time as diverse in appearance as here.

TOP / LEFT **South garden;** *tsukiyama* **crossing into the sea** ⑤   RIGHT **Circles of gravel accented by snow; Hōrai stone setting in back**

Kishiwada-jō, 1953

Mirei Shigemori's layout suggests the castle's old fortification walls and at the same time stages a battle scene from Chinese mythology. The garden's location on the site of a military castle is what inspired Shigemori to use his stone settings to refer to Zhuge Liang's eight-fold battlecamp formation. The garden is stylistically a *karesansui* design that slopes up toward the middle, where the stone setting representing the captain's Central Camp takes the main stage.

HISTORY   The castle at its current location was built in 1615 when Koide Harima-no-kami Hidemasa took up residence in the area as its ruler. Soon after Okabe Minō-no-kami Nobukatsu came to power in 1640, he built a moat and a stone wall around the castle. From that point on, Kishiwada Castle developed together with the castle town. After the Meiji Restoration in 1868, the government abolished the old feudal domains and reorganized Japan into new geopolitical units called prefectures. Eventually Mr. Okabe, Kishiwada Castle's last owner, donated the property to the city.

In early spring 1953 Tarō Fukumoto, the mayor of Kishiwada, proposed the construction of a garden at the castle. On 30 June he asked Mirei Shigemori to prepare a design proposal for the garden. The plans were finished by 27 July, and work on the garden started on 13 October. Prince Takamatsu visited the site once during construction on 16 November, a

View across garden toward castle ❾ to ❶

big day for everybody involved. Work progressed quickly and the garden was completed by 20 December. The castle tower, which had been destroyed by lightning in 1827, was finally rebuilt the following year, in 1954.

Three planes rising toward the center ❸ ❷

DESCRIPTION The site is enclosed by an impressive Momoyama period (1568–1600) stone wall and at 1,650 square meters is comparatively large. The only access to this manmade island is from the northwest via a bridge across the moat. The castle tower is located to the southeast, opposite the entrance.

View from castle ❾ ❶ ❻ ❷

Regarding his design intention Shigemori notes: "Castles are supposed to last forever, and the garden attached to such a castle should be designed in the same spirit. This is what I was most concerned about; hence, I made a garden from stone. But I was also inspired by the fact that this is the garden of a fortress, for it is located in the heart of the castle grounds. So in designing the garden's layout as an abstraction of the old fortification system I am referring to the Muromachi period's organization of the site."[16] It seems then that durability and the potential for abstraction were the main reasons Mirei Shigemori chose the *karesansui* style for this garden design. The sharp-angled lines of low walls in the sand, depicting the layout of the old moats, is the image a bird would have seen some three hundred years ago from high up in the sky.

Concerning the stone arrangements in the garden Shigemori continues: "I designed the arrangement of the stone settings with respect to the eight-fold battlecamp formation of Zhuge Liang. This formation has a main camp in the center with eight subcamps surrounding it. These were called Heaven ➎, Earth ➌, Wind ➒, Cloud ➐, Dragon ➑, Tiger ➍, Phoenix ➋, and Snake ➏."[17] The names of these historical camps, originally related to Chinese mythology, are what Shigemori used as the chief inspiration for his stone settings in the garden.

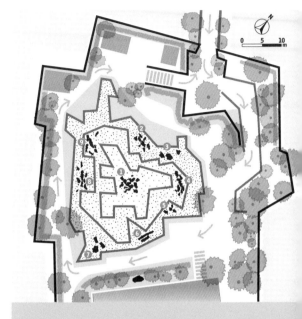

FULL NAME
Kishiwada-jō Hachi-jin no Niwa (Kishiwada Castle Garden of Eight Battle Formations).

LOCATION ➋ 🅰
Kishiwada City in Ōsaka Prefecture; 15 km south of Ōsaka.

CATEGORY
A castle garden in *karesansui* style.

THEME
A famous eight-fold battlecamp formation set within low walls that abstractly represent the castle's old fortification.

WHEN TO VISIT
The castle grounds are open to the public and the garden can be enjoyed year round. If you visit on 14 or 15 September you can see the Danjiri Festival that passes by the castle every year.

In addition to the eight peripheral camps, there is the captain's Central Camp ➊, depicted by the main stone setting in the middle of the garden. It is composed of several large upright stones and can be viewed from all sides. The peripheral stone settings each consist of from two to nine stones, depending on their theme. The Camp of the Dragon stone setting ❸ in the south part, for example, uses nine stones to represent a dragon rising up to heaven through black clouds. The Camp of the Snake stone setting ❻ in the east part, on the other hand, consists of only two stones representing a long snake. The stones, by the way, are Mirei Shigemori's favorite *aoishi*, in this case from Okinoshima, a small island near Shikoku.

The Central Camp stone setting ❶ sits on the highest level in the center of the garden. The Camp of the Tiger ❷ and the Camp of the Wind ❹ are located below on the middle level, and the rest of the camps are on the lowest level. The jagged lines marking the edges of the three different levels meet in various angles and create a variety of shapes among themselves. Sometimes they are almost parallel and sometimes not, thus forming triangles or even diamond-shaped spaces. Each level is thirty centimeters higher than the previous, sloping up as it approaches the center.

Unlike most other *karesansui* gardens, the example here can be appreciated from any viewpoint; the scene naturally changes as you walk around the edge of the garden. The design can also be enjoyed from the top floor of the castle tower, with its commanding view of the garden and the surrounding urban landscape. Another distinctive feature comes from Shigemori's notion that people should be able to walk on the wall lines and thereby approach the center without stepping onto the sand. He notes: "If you walk on the outer line, you can jump to the next inner line when the two get close. And then finally you can step onto the innermost line and get even closer to the center." Not only did he think people should enter the garden, he even thought of it as a space for events: "I planned for the possibility of using this garden as an exhibition space and even as a theater. And as the city was planning a library in the castle tower I thought the garden might also be used as an outdoor reading space. So even though the design of this garden seems very simple, it in fact allows for many different uses."[18] This is how the garden at Kishiwada Castle became the first *kare-*

Linear stone walls to walk on!

sansui garden in Japan to be used as an exhibition and performance space. Two years after the garden's opening a number of metal sculptures were displayed during an outdoor exhibition.[19] And during that same event Yūgo Shigemori, Mirei Shigemori's only daughter, gave a traditional Japanese dance performance on the garden stage. Mirei Shigemori produced his daughter's performance, and who would have guessed that the theme of the dance was the straight and the curved line!

"Rikyū said that until you become thirty, you have to study the way the master orders you. Then when you become thirty, 'east is west and mountain is valley.' So if the master teaches you to go east, you have to go west, if he says mountain you have to study valley. Until you are thirty you have to absorb the master's teachings, but after that you have to use your own mind to create your own work.
If you follow the master's word your whole life you cannot do creative work."[20]

INTERPRETATION The stone settings are without a doubt an important part of this garden, but the angled lines are really the main feature. They represent a revolutionary addition to the traditional vocabulary of the *karesansui* style garden,

LEFT **Points and lines of stone on a plane of gravel**   RIGHT **Geometry and natural shapes: angled lines contrast with stone settings**

which for centuries had been made from just sand and rocks alone. The linear walls were built in stone first and foremost to make them last: lines raked in sand fade away rather fast from wind and weather, but these lines will remain as long as the concrete holds the stones in place.

However, when designing this garden, Shigemori did not have only longevity in mind. He was also striving to create his own contemporary Japanese garden. In his words: "As you can see on the plan, the garden is composed of three stone lines, which are angling back and forth. I took reference to the old layout of the fortress and transferred it into a modern artistic expression. . . . My main idea was to create a layout referring to the original Kishiwada Castle from an aerial view, something that had never been done so far."[21] Just being a contemporary garden was not quite enough; it had to be new as well. And looking at the result, we have to say that a *karesansui* garden like this had never been seen before in Japan.

And yet there is still another aspect to the folded angular lines in the garden of Kishiwada Castle. Shigemori had a vision of the future, in which people were seeing gardens and landscapes more often from the air. He explains: "People in the future will probably appreciate the garden in ways different from how people presently do. This garden is supposed to last for more than a thousand years, so it is not good enough to think about how people in today's world appreciate such a garden. Technology will develop and people will be using planes and helicopters more frequently, in which case the garden will often be seen from above, high up in the sky."[22] Admittedly this is a rather rare aspect to be taken into account for the design of a Japanese garden, but in the case of the garden of Kishiwada Castle it is a clear argument for the use of the strong line. Mere planes of gravel and points of stone would not have been easily detectable from up in the air. It must be one of the ironies of history that, forty years after its establishment, this garden is just a stone's throw away from the new Kansai Airport built on a manmade island in Ōsaka Bay.

A garden made to last: sand and rocks, plus linear walls ◉

Zuihō-in, 1961

The south garden at Zuihō-in depicts an impressive coastal mountain, with the whole scene extending from the turbulent waters of the ocean to a protected inland bay. The north garden features a hidden Christian cross in the form of a stone setting, an allusion to the suppression of Christianity in medieval Japan.

HISTORY Zuihō-in is one of twenty-two subtemples within Kyōto's Daitoku-ji temple complex and was founded in 1546 by Sōrin Ōtomo, who at the time was a *daimyō* (feudal lord) in Kyūshū and a devoted follower of the Rinzai school of Zen Buddhism.[23] He later became a devout Christian and was baptized at the age of forty-eight by a Jesuit father. The current *hōjō* dates back to 1535 and is registered as an Important Cultural Asset.

In 1960 the Kyōto Garden Association began raising money from their members for the construction of a garden to commemorate the Association's thirtieth anniversary.[24] A committee was established whose purpose was to find a suitable site. The ideal location would be at a well-visited temple, would be neither too big nor too small, and would ideally be adjacent to a temple dating from the Momoyama period (1568–1600) that was still in good condition. The committee members visited many temples and after a long discussion selected Zuihō-in for the commemorative garden. As Mirei Shigemori was then president of the Association, he naturally took

Mt. Hōrai and turbulent ocean waters, eastward view ➊

up the project as his own and drew up a design for the garden. Construction started on 16 April 1961 and was finished by 11 May for the temple's four-hundredth anniversary. The stone setting in the south garden was done in only two days, 16–17 April, and by 19 April most of the south garden was complete. To coincide with the temple's own celebrations, the Garden Association's present to itself was actually finished a year early. The thirtieth anniversary of the Kyōto Garden Association was thus celebrated the following year in June 1962.

DESCRIPTION The south garden is long and narrow and extends along the southern border of the property. Inspired by the temple's name, Zuihō 瑞峯, which translates as "Blissful Mountain," the garden's main focal point

is a tall stone setting, symbolizing the legendary sacred peak of Mt. Hōrai. From there a ridge extends down and out into the sea, eventually taking the form of a low stone peninsula ❶. The ocean of sand is always raked rather dramatically, creating the appearance of a rough sea at the foot of the mountain. The base around the main stone setting, as well as the garden section to the west, is mostly covered with moss. In the western section there are no stone settings, apart from a few stepping stones, giving the landscape here more the feel of a quiet bay ❷. To screen the entire coastal scene from the neighboring prop-

Stepping stones crossing inland bay ❷

erty, a long *karikomi* was planted as a backdrop, part of which takes the form of a double hedge.

Further north, squeezed in between the *hōjō* and the teahouse, is a rectangular tea garden with a stone basin. The initial design by Mirei Shigemori, a very abstract all-stone garden with diagonal geometric lines, must have been too extreme for the temple. Over the course of some renovation work on the building in the early seventies it was replaced by a more conventional tea garden with many plantings.

Behind the *hōjō* is the mysterious Garden of the Cross. Located on the north side of the building, it consists basically of the same elements as its counterpart to the south, but here the stone setting symbolizes a Christian cross ❸ in reference to the founder's conversion to that religion. It is set in a sea of gravel and balanced by two different hedges and a low *tsukiyama* covered

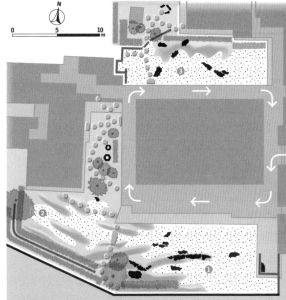

FULL NAME
Zuihō-in Teien (Garden of the Blissful Mountain Hut); Dokuza no Niwa (Garden of Solitary Meditation, south of the *hōjō*); Kanmin no Niwa (Quietly Sleeping Garden, or Garden of the Cross, north garden).

LOCATION ❸卍
Kita-ku in Kyōto; located in the extensive Daitoku-ji temple complex in the northern part of the city.

CATEGORY
Two *karesansui* gardens.

THEME
A mountain-seaside landscape (south garden) and a hidden Christian cross (north garden), both dedicated to Sōrin Ōtomo, a Christian *daimyō*.

WHEN TO VISIT
The garden is open to the public, and since most of the background planting is evergreen it is attractive in any season. The moss is at its best after the rainy season in late June and into July. Avoid visiting during peak season and national holidays, when the garden gets crowded.

in moss. A short stepping-stone path leads to another tea garden further north behind the hedge.

"A garden that will stand the test of scrutiny is not just one whose material qualities will endure. Instead, is it a garden that, even as people's outlooks change over time, is suffused with permanent beauty." [25]

INTERPRETATION Zuihō-in is the quintessential Zen garden. The south garden is even named Dokuza no Niwa 独坐の庭, or "Garden of Solitary Meditation." The garden's main purpose is thus to offer a place to sit alone in meditation, in front of an impressive landscape. According to Zen, being in solitude in this kind of environment helps a human being become conscious of his existence in the world. [26]

In terms of design, the south garden of Zuihō-in is perhaps the most traditional among the gardens presented in this book. Although much abstracted, the design depicts a seaside landscape in a relatively naturalistic way. A little closer to Mirei Shigemori's later approach to the *karesansui* garden is the north garden at Zuihō-in; here he is actively looking for other themes that can be depicted using the elements of the dry landscape garden.

The north garden is named Kanmin no Niwa 閑眠の庭, actually meaning the "Quietly Sleeping Garden" but more often simply referred to as the Garden of the Cross. The name hints at the fact that with regard to Christianity things were only quiet and peaceful on the surface in Japan. The Japanese gov-

LEFT **Hidden Christian cross stone setting in north garden ❸**   RIGHT **View west from protected inland bay ❷**

ernment in the 1600s had forbidden Christianity and attempted to stamp out all visible signs of its practice. Over the next 250 years, Christianity in Japan flourished undercover and in secret. One could only recognize it if one knew it was there. The same is now true for Shigemori's stone setting in the form of a cross; you can only see it if you know it is there.

Part of "Mt. Hōrai" stone setting; westward view ❶

Another interesting point regarding Zuihō-in is that Shigemori didn't hesitate to integrate Buddhist and Christian references into the designs for the gardens of a single temple. Similarly, in the garden at Fukuchi-in, described later in this book, he incorporates Shintō and Buddhist references even into the very same garden space. All this points to a refreshing degree of religious tolerance that is often found in Japanese culture.

To build a garden at one of Daitoku-ji's famous old temples and on top of that as a commemorative work, all paid for by the members of the Kyōto Garden Association, placed considerable pressure on Mirei Shigemori to produce an outstanding composition. He notes: "There are many famous and old gardens at Daitoku-ji, so this one couldn't possibly be just an ordinary classic style. If it were, the Garden Association would lose face. I had to build the absolutely best garden I could, even though it was all-volunteer work for me and was also on a very tight construction budget. To be able to make a garden at Daitoku-ji was a milestone in my life, so I did my best to leave something interesting behind and put a lot of effort into the job."[27]

The result at Zuihō-in speaks for itself. The Mt. Hōrai stone setting is certainly among Shigemori's best and most powerful works. The constant stream of visitors that the temple gets is ample testimony to the good reputation the garden has made for itself.

Waves of gravel, accented by snow ❶

Sumiyoshi Jinja, 1966

According to Mirei Shigemori, the shrine garden as its own distinct style does not yet exist. He thus selected the *karesansui* style, with its design rooted in the ancient Shintō *iwakura*, as the most appropriate form for this garden. With an undulating concrete line Shigemori introduces the wave to the ocean of sand, making an unmistakable contemporary accent.

HISTORY   In 1081 a spirit was brought to Suminoe from Sumiyoshi Taisha in Ōsaka, and the local community built Sumiyoshi Jinja for its worship. The shrine was restored once in 1467. Matsudaira Yasunobu, who governed the area at that time, dedicated a bell to the shrine.[28] The tower for it still exists, and a replica of the original bell has recently been installed. Other than that only the shrine, dating from before the Meiji Restoration (1868), and the main hall remain to this day. The latter is a fine piece of Edo-period (1600–1868) architecture and was originally the shrine's guesthouse. It is currently used as the office.

Masao Nonoguchi, head of the Shrine Association in the 1960s, worked hard to maintain the shrine and wanted to see it flourish again. That is why in March 1966 Mirei Shigemori was formally asked to make a garden at Sumiyoshi Taisha. Shigemori directed the construction in person and completed the work by July of that year.[29]

Seaside landscape with *shakkei* using hills of Hyōgo Prefecture

Proposing a shrine-garden style: *karesansui* with a twist

Today the widow of the former priest keeps the building and the garden up, with the help of the shrine's supporters. The white sand is weeded and the raked pattern redrawn every year for the Minazuki Festival at the end of July.

DESCRIPTION The garden is located to the north of the main building and was for a long time enclosed by trees. In recent years much of the vegetation has been removed, opening up a view to the surrounding landscape. The garden's shape is a perfect rectangle, with earthen walls to the east and the north and a bamboo fence on the west side.

The god enshrined in Sumiyoshi Jinja is the *kami* of the sea. This inspired Mirei Shigemori to depict a seaside landscape in the garden, despite its location amid the hills of Hyōgo Prefecture. Shigemori drew three winding lines on a plane of gravel and contrasted them with fifteen stones. The lines are made of white concrete and symbolize waves washing up to the beach. The closer they get to the building, the imagined shore, the more undulation they show. In the ocean of white sand, brought in from Kyōto, Shigemori designed small islands of moss, mostly adjacent to one of the lines. The stones, set in a 7-5-3 combination, are his favorite *aoishi* from Shikoku. Between the waves is a small longish stone ❶, floating alone in the sand, representing a boat en route to the islands of the immortals.

On the west side of the garden, where there is no earthen wall, Shigemori created a bamboo fence with a theme also connected to the beachside scene. The original design depicted a fisherman's net hung up to dry, albeit in a rather abstract fashion. Unfortunately this unusual fence has recently been replaced by a much more simple version.

"One should not just reproduce the traditional gardens of olden times, but should study those works well and then refer to them when making a contemporary garden. To refer to and to imitate are two very different things." [30]

INTERPRETATION Even in the 1960s there were few shrines with a distinctive garden, so Mirei Shigemori was very interested in working on such a project and further exploring the possibilities for a more defined shrine garden style. Well aware that the tradi-

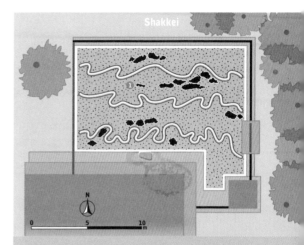

FULL NAME
Sumiyoshi Jinja Teien, Suminoe no Niwa (Suminoe Garden).

LOCATION
Sasayama City in Hyōgo Prefecture; 32 km west of Kyōto.

CATEGORY
A shrine garden in *karesansui* style.

THEME
A shrine building at a seaside location, the ocean and waves washing ashore.

WHEN TO VISIT
The garden is not open to the general public. It is good to view any time of the year but is probably in the best shape right after the Minazuki Festival, which takes place on 31 July. Write ahead to the shrine for permission to see the garden.

tion of the early *karesansui* garden, which Zen had adopted, was deeply rooted in ancient Shintō, he felt it would be well suited to a contemporary shrine garden design.[31] And since the idea of a seaside scene was in such strong thematic and aesthetic contrast to the hilly landscape surrounding the shrine, only the *karesansui* style, Shigemori realized, would allow the garden to achieve the degree of abstraction needed to make the contrast work.

TOP **Waves washing up to shore; westward view**   RIGHT **Islands of moss, islands of stone**

Boat stone between two waves ❶

When Shigemori arranged the stones as islands out in a sea of sand, he for one thing referred to the Taoist idea of the islands of the immortals as well as the god of the sea. But the stones also stand for the original Shintō concept of the *iwakura*, a purified and godly rock. By establishing this connection between the god of the sea and the *kami* of the *iwakura*, he could again validate the co-existence of different religious beliefs, a tradition that Sumiyoshi Jinja had followed over much of the past nine hundred years.

Clearly this garden features the boldest line design among all of Mirei Shigemori's works.[32] In no other garden did he create an independent line with such vigor and vividness: three waves made from white concrete, getting stronger and more coiled as they wash up to the shore. The result is a very unique shrine garden: flamboyant as a design but at the same time well rooted in history and place.

NEXT SPREAD LEFT **Winding lines on a plane of raked sand**   NEXT SPREAD RIGHT **White concrete contrasts well with weathered rock**

Yūrin no Niwa, (1969) 2002

Originally designed for the building of the Association of Kimono Manufacturers in Kyōto, the layout of the garden refers to a local kimono famous for its colorful *noshi* bundle design. *Noshi* are auspicious strips of dried fish or seaweed that are tied in a cluster as a symbol of good luck and unlimited happiness. The garden was saved from destruction and recently rebuilt in Mirei Shigemori's hometown.

HISTORY   Relocating buildings and gardens is not uncommon in Japan, but among the gardens in this book Yūrin no Niwa is the only one to have had two homes. The garden's history began in April 1968 when the Association of Kimono Manufacturers in Kyōto decided to build an exhibition hall and hired an architect named Tomiie to work out a plan. In August of the same year the Matsui Kensetsu Construction Company won the contract for the realization of the building, and on 23 August a groundbreaking ceremony was held. While construction was underway, some of the Association's board members visited Mirei Shigemori and asked him for a design for the garden. Shigemori drew up a proposal, which he presented to the Association. He got the commission and finished his drawings by the end of the year. Construction of the garden was completed on 29 March 1969, and this was followed by a big inaugural celebration the next day.

Courtyard with *noshi* bundle design viewed from second floor

Thirty years later, in December 1999, the exhibition hall was slated for demolition to make way for a new apartment building. Toshio Iwamoto, a gardener and one of Shigemori's later students, rescued most of the garden's materials. More than eighty truckloads of stone and rock were stored in Okayama until a new location for the garden was found. As chance would have it, Mirei Shigemori's hometown, now part of Kibichūō-chō, was building a new town hall. Not surprisingly, the town took this as an opportunity to bring home a garden designed by one of its most prominent native sons. The new building was thus designed to accommodate the shape of Shigemori's garden, and during construction the salvaged pieces of stone were assembled on a nearby trial site. Iwamoto and his team finished the second incarnation of Yūrin no Niwa on 4 October 2002. For the official opening on 10 November, Tadakazu Saitō came and gave a lecture. A former employee of Mirei Shigemori, Saitō had been in charge of the garden's first construction thirty-four years earlier in Kyōto.

DESCRIPTION   This courtyard in pond-garden style consists of a nearly square space and an adjacent rectangular space, at the conjunction of which is a covered corridor. Where in Kyōto the stepping stones connected the

exhibition hall with lecture rooms and offices across the pond, in the new setting the stones are a shortcut from the offices to the library and the maintenance facilities. Originally the garden's size was 410 square meters; the second version is just slightly larger.

Regarding his design intention Shigemori states the following: "When I designed this garden

18th-century kimono with *noshi* bundle design; Important Cultural Property, Yūzenshi-kai, Kyōto

I wanted to create something that felt very modern and that was completely out of the ordinary."[33] With his client being a very artistic group of craftsmen, it was the right moment to create a highly inventive and abstract garden. No wonder the outcome is colorful and, of course, modern.

A pond, the design of which is based on a kimono pattern, dominates the center of this space. The shallow water nicely highlights the red stones from Tanba and the blue ones from the island of Shikoku. The triangular area in the southwest corner is a *karesansui* garden, and so are most of the southern and eastern sections of the courtyard. Some of the blue stones set on pebble-covered mounds in the pond naturally represent islands in the

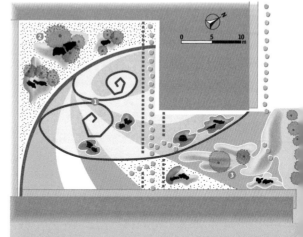

FULL NAME
Yūrin no Niwa (Yūrin's Garden).

LOCATION ⑤ ⽊
Kibichūō-chō in Kaga-gun, Okayama Prefecture; 45 km northwest of Okayama City.

CATEGORY
A pond garden.

THEME
A *noshi*, or auspicious bundle, alluding to a famous kimono pattern from the Edo period.

WHEN TO VISIT
The garden is now located at the Kibichūō-chō Town Hall, a public space that is accessible year round. A visit could coincide with Yoshikawa's impressive Tōban Festival, which takes place every year on 27 October.

ocean. Two narrow white lines ❶ made of cut stone extend out of the pond all the way into the paving of the eastern part of the garden, thereby making a secure connection between the dry and wet areas. The *tsukiyama* in the southwest corner ❷ is planted with a large pine tree and covered with moss, as is the longish peninsula in the northern section ❸ that represents the famous landscape of Amanohashidate.[34] Shigemori designed this garden to be admired from any corner of the site as well as from above.

INTERPRETATION The garden's main feature is a pond inspired by the design of a *noshi* bundle on a famous eighteenth-century kimono.[35] This piece of clothing still exists; classified as an Important Cultural Property, it stands as a symbol of the high level of craftsmanship that silk dyeing had reached in Kyōto. The spirals of thin white lines represent the ribbons that hold the bundle together; the wider, colorful paving symbolizes the *noshi* strips. The pattern successfully occupies the ground plane, an effect much used in recent Western landscape architecture, for example in the works of Peter Walker.

"I would not care to make a garden a certain way just because my master had taught me so or because of strong family tradition. The effect of doing so would be that all gardens eventually become stereotypical. It was always a principle in my work to not make one garden the same as another." [36]

By referencing this famous kimono Shigemori gives the garden a strong local connection, one that everybody in the Association of Kimono Manufacturers can relate to. Taking one of the client's main icons as an inspiration for his garden was a very shrewd move and must have helped considerably with getting this very abstract design approved and actually built.

The garden's name, by the way, is composed of the first syllable 友 of Yūzensai 友禅斉, the man who developed the silk-dyeing technique, and the second syllable 琳 of Kōrin 光琳, a famous painter said to have inspired Yūzensai's textile designs. Shigemori saw these avant-garde kimono patterns, among them the *noshi* bundle design, as a collaborative work of Yūzensai and Kōrin, hence the name. The Association's members liked the idea so much that they not only agreed to call the garden Yūrin no Niwa, but even decided to name the entire complex the Yūrin Exhibition Hall.

Pebbles with covered corridor in rear

NEXT SPREAD LEFT **Peninsula with pine tree and moss representing Amanohashidate**   NEXT SPREAD RIGHT **Spiral as center focal point of pool**

Tenrai-an, 1969

In 1969 Mirei Shigemori gave the teahouse he had built as a young boy together with his father to the town of Kayo-chō (now Kibichūō-chō). The new location demanded a few adjustments as well as a new garden, all of which was included in this gift to his hometown. Waves and sand banks, inspired by the neighboring shrine that is dedicated to the god of the sea, are the theme of Shigemori's avant-garde tea garden design.

HISTORY The history of this site really begins when Mirei Shigemori takes up the study of the tea ceremony at the age of fifteen. Soon he wishes to have his own teahouse, which he designs and builds at the age of eighteen with the help of his father, a gifted amateur carpenter. For the teahouse's dedication he invites his tea teacher, Mrs. Aizawa, as the main guest. Shigemori makes frequent use of the teahouse until 1929, when he decides to move to Kyōto.

By 1968 the house of Shigemori's childhood had deteriorated so much that it needed to be taken down, but the adjacent teahouse was still in rather good shape and hence was saved. A man named Nishitani, an old friend, suggested that Shigemori donate the teahouse to the town of Kayo-chō. A suitable piece of property was soon found between the village shrine and the town hall. The relocation of the structure required the addition of

Contemporary tea garden or walk-on sculpture? ❸

a *mizuya*, a space for preparing the tea uten-
sils, as well as a waiting area for the guests. As
the town didn't have the money to pay for all
this, Shigemori had no choice but to cover the
cost himself. On 29 March 1968 he submitted
a design proposal to the town, but construction didn't start until 15 August of the following year. By the middle of September 1969 the
stepping stones were already in place and the

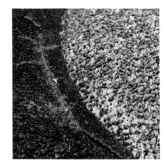

White waves and red sand banks

teahouse was half finished. On 13 October the red and white sand for the
tsukiyama was being prepared. Most of the construction was finished by 20
October 1969. The opening tea ceremony was held on 28–29 October with
more than 300 people attending.

DESCRIPTION The garden is located on the property of Yoshikawa
Hachimangū shrine, which is dedicated to the god of the sea. It is this shrine
deity that inspired Mirei Shigemori to design a garden representing ocean
waves and sand banks, suggested abstractly by red and white concrete. The
wave of white concrete originates near the teahouse and subsequently turns
into a spiral shape, jutting out into the ocean. Most of the red concrete is
mounded, just as natural sand banks are in the sea. Further out the waves
widen and stretch all the way from east to west. Thus as one looks from
the teahouse into the distance, the waves and the sand banks seem to fold
into each other. The teahouse itself sits on a rectangular platform of red
concrete, connected by stepping stones to the waiting area ❷ and eventually the entrance ❶. A visitor walking up to the teahouse passes though the
middle gate ❸ at a bamboo fence before entering the hut through a small,
low door. The teahouse itself is in the center of the northern section of the
property and faces south, while the waiting area is in the southwest corner
and faces east. Worked into the fence pattern is the Chinese character for

"sky" or "heaven" 天, pronounced *ten*, the first syllable of the tea garden's name, Tenrai-an.

"I try to capture the sense of modern times in the movement of the line. It is the very same pebble beach (of earlier times), but to it I bring a modern spirit using brightness, speedy movement, and a lively curve." [37]

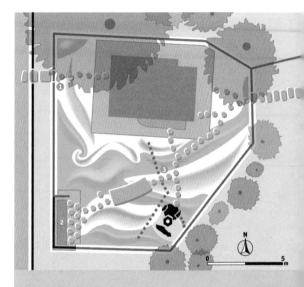

FULL NAME
Tenrai-an Teien (Garden at the Hermitage for the Enjoyment of Nature's Sounds).

LOCATION 🌀 🅰
Kibichūō-chō in Kaga-gun, Okayama Prefecture; 45 km north-west of Okayama City; next to Yoshikawa Hachimangū shrine.

CATEGORY
A contemporary tea garden.

THEME
The waves and sand banks of the sea.

WHEN TO VISIT
This tea garden, located right next to Yoshikawa Hachimangū shrine, is usually not open to the public. For permission to see the garden, contact the nearby Shigemori Mirei Museum in advance. As with Yūrin no Niwa, a visit to the town could coincide with the Tōban Festival.

INTERPRETATION The traditional tea garden in Japan is a calm, rather green space with a lot of planting, ideally suggesting an austere hermitage deep in the mountains, hidden away in a dark valley. But according to Mirei Shigemori, anybody could create such a tea garden, and certainly many of this type exist all over Japan. As a man devoted to making contemporary gardens, Shigemori resolved to create a tea garden without using a single plant, and on top of that decided to make it using colored concrete.

For this, probably his most extreme tea garden design, Shigemori at first gives two very practical reasons: "At the northwest corner of this garden is a big old fir tree whose leaves are too small to be kept out of the

NEXT SPREAD LEFT **Possibly Japan's most avant-garde tea garden**   NEXT SPREAD RIGHT **Sculpted landscape of mounded red and white concrete**

Middle gate ❸ with *tsukubai* to left and waiting area in back

sand, and this really makes it impossible to use sand in this garden. Furthermore, there is no one to take care of the moss. This is when I realized that the only design that would work in these conditions is a very abstract tea garden, not the ordinary kind."[38] Obviously, over the years Shigemori had grown skilled at selling his avant-garde ideas with very practical arguments, knowing this tactic would get him much further than philosophical discussions. But in the case of Tenrai-an he was in a very comfortable position anyway, being almost his own client. Paying all of the costs clearly gave him the freedom to design the garden the way he wanted to. And knowing that the local government would keep the garden in good condition, Shigemori was confident that his work would be well preserved for the future. So he went wild and tried something that he wouldn't be able to do anywhere else. His tea garden in reality is less a garden and more a walk-on sculpture. It is somehow reminiscent of some of Isamu Noguchi's later works, many of which are similarly sculpted landscapes.[39]

Mirei Shigemori created a provocative design like the one at Tenrai-an primarily due to his conviction that the Japanese tea garden needed to modernize: "Teahouses and tea gardens should not just remain traditional. Tea itself is an aesthetic microcosm of all art, and it always continues to develop and be connected to the changes of our own daily lives."[40] So in actuality this garden is a built statement advocating the continuous renewal of Japanese garden art, especially that of the tea garden.

Spiral wave jutting into the ocean, seen from the fence

Sekizō-ji, 1972

For two reasons, Sekizō-ji represents a milestone in the development of the *karesansui* garden. First, it does not imitate or recall a mythical landscape or a painting of such a landscape, and second, it uses four colors of gravel instead of one. With this garden Mirei Shigemori is deliberately testing the limits of what a dry landscape garden can be in Japan.

HISTORY The fact that the old name of the temple is Iwakura-ji, together with the large *iwakura* visible up the hillside behind the site, suggests that this location has been a place of worship for a very long time. The recorded history says that Sekizō-ji[41] had originally been built in the forest behind the current building, but that it had burned down and been rebuilt in 1644 by the priest Tōseki at the current location.

The *iwakura* here, as the name implies, is a rock that the ancient Japanese people admired as a god or as a site of a god's immanence. It was believed that on this stone outcropping the *kami* descended at certain times of the year, thus connecting this locale to the world of the gods. But sometime in the twentieth century people forgot all about the *iwakura* behind the temple; trees grew, and little by little the stone outcropping was hidden.

View from Black Tortoise ❶ to Red Phoenix ❸, with *shishin* 四神, "four gods," written on the bamboo fence ❺

In 1971 supporters of the temple began to discuss making a garden in front of the main hall. Masao Nonoguchi, who owned a brewery in the nearby town of Tanba Taki, introduced Mirei Shigemori's work to the temple's priest.[42] About this same time, the trees that had grown up around the *iwakura* were removed and the entire stone outcropping was suddenly revealed. On 6 July 1971, Mirei Shigemori was officially commissioned to design a new garden for Sekizō-ji. He drew up a project plan on 25 September of the same year, but construction didn't start until March of the following year, as the requisite fundraising took some time. On 22–23 March Shigemori was on site for the placement of the four stone arrangements. Construction was completed on 14 May 1972, resulting in the first garden in Japan ever to be based on the concept of *shishin sōō*.[43]

Overview from southwest corner ⑤, with *seki* 石, "stone," written on the bamboo fence in back ⑥

DESCRIPTION Inspired by the newly revealed *iwakura*, Mirei Shigemori decided to make a garden for the gods, basing it on the ancient Chinese concept of *shishin sōō*, the four gods who protect the four heavenly directions.[44] The four gods, represented by four stone settings, chase each other counterclockwise around a circle in front of the main hall. Each stone setting is associated with one of the four directions:

EAST is symbolized by the dragon ❹ and is associated with the color blue. The dragon also represents the element of wood and is considered the earth guardian. In the east square of the garden are long stones placed to suggest the Blue Dragon with surrounding blue sand.

SOUTH is symbolized by the phoenix ❸ and is associated with the color red. The phoenix also represents the fire element and is considered a guardian against it. In the south square a Red Phoenix stone setting is spreading its wings in a plane of red sand.

WEST is symbolized by the tiger ❷ and is associated with the color white. The tiger also represents the element of metal and is considered the wind guardian. In the west square the stone setting imitates a White Tiger with a bed of white sand around it.

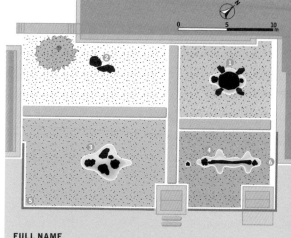

FULL NAME
Masshō Honzan Sekizō-ji, Shishin Sōō no Niwa (Garden of Four Gods).

LOCATION ❼ 🗺
Ichijima-chō in Hikami-gun, Hyōgo Prefecture; 5 km south of Fukuchiyama.

CATEGORY
A temple garden in *karesansui* style.

THEME
Design based on the concept of *shishin sōō*, the four gods who protect the four heavenly directions around a specific land area.

WHEN TO VISIT
The gardens at Sekizō-ji are open to the public and accessible year round. Because the *iwakura* behind the temple is up a steep forest road, access is a bit more difficult after a heavy rain.

Red Phoenix with four colors of gravel at path intersection

NORTH is symbolized by the tortoise ❶ and is associated with the color black. The tortoise also represents the water element and is considered the water guardian. In the north square a Black Tortoise stone setting is placed amid a plane of black sand.

Taking all four quarters together we are looking at a 4-2-5-7 stone arrangement. The idea is that the *kami* first descends from the *iwakura* to the Black Tortoise (north), as it is geographically the closest. Then it continues to the White Tiger (west) and on to the Red Phoenix (south). Next the god jumps from the Phoenix to the Blue Dragon (east), and at the end all four gods perform a dance while chasing each other around in a circle.

The system of paths in the garden cuts the plane in front of the main hall into four sectors, of which the northern and the eastern are the smallest. One path leads straight from the gate toward the main hall. About half way, and slightly off center, two more paths branch away in the direction of the two smaller buildings on each side of the main hall.

As you face the garden while standing in front of the main hall, you can see Chinese characters that read as *shishin* 四神 visible on the bamboo fence to the right ❺, just behind the Red Phoenix. Carrying the meaning "four gods," the graphic directly refers to the garden's main theme. To the left of the gate, and continuing on around the corner from the little bell tower, the bamboo fence features the Chinese character pronounced *seki* 石 ❻, the first character of the temple's name Sekizō-ji 石像寺, a reference to the temple's origin at the *iwakura* high up behind the building.

"If what the gods made is nature, then the garden is the part that the gods forgot to make. So it is up to us to take the place of the gods and make gardens. We ourselves must become the gods." [45]

INTERPRETATION The garden at Sekizō-ji essentially consists of a single large plane defined by the buildings surrounding it on three sides and the fence that marks its southeastern border. It is further divided into four subplanes, as suggested by the concept of *shishin sōō*.

Each subplane is dominated by a stone setting that acts as its central focal point, and each has a designated color that is applied to its rocks, gravel, and paving stones. Choosing *shishin sōō* as the basis for the garden thus led Shigemori to create a remarkable and significant design innovation, the first time in the history of the Japanese garden that a garden maker has

LEFT **Red Phoenix** ❸ **and fence with "four gods" characters in rear**   RIGHT **Bamboo fence with knot and Blue Dragon** ❹ **in front**

used four different colors of gravel in a single dry landscape garden.

Here, as he did at the garden at Tenrai-an, Shigemori uses the bamboo fence as an additional plane to draw on. This time he includes a reference to the garden's main theme as well as a link to its origin. Both are obvious statements for those who know the meaning of this garden, but for everyone else they serve as an aid to better understanding the place. Here also, after Tenrai-an, is the second example of writing or a font being used as an

Black Tortoise ❶ swimming away toward White Tiger ❷

ornament on a fence to add further layers of meaning to the garden space.

The *karesansui* plane offers the ideal platform for the *shishin sōō* idea. In no other style of Japanese garden would a design with this theme have come out so clearly. But Shigemori had another good reason to make a *karesansui* garden here: his quest for a new style of temple garden is another aspect of his enduring commitment to the contemporary garden. He notes: "This garden is not a *karesansui* garden just because there is no water in it. It depicts the ancient faith in god in a contemporary design appropriate for modern times. As such it departs from the concept of the conventional *karesansui* garden, which usually imitates natural landscapes. Therefore Sōō no Niwa should really be seen as a new type of *karesansui* garden."[46] Once more the *karesansui* garden's great potential for abstraction led Mirei Shigemori to experiment with stone and gravel; the result is a distinctive use of geometry and color, this time in the garden of a temple in the Japanese countryside.

Whorls produced by swimming Black Tortoise

Hōkoku Jinja, 1972

Hōkoku Jinja was built in memory of Toyotomi Hideyoshi, so the gourd, which is the famous warrior's trademark, offered itself as a memorable and recognizable garden motif. Combining a large *tsukiyama* of red-brown concrete and powerful stone settings, the garden offers a new interpretation of the *karesansui* style and as such is a milestone in Mirei Shigemori's work.

HISTORY   Toyotomi Hideyoshi, the great Japanese general who united Japan, died at Fushimi Castle, south of Kyōto, at the age of sixty-two in 1598. That same year Hōkoku Jinja was founded in his memory. The warrior's soul became a god after his death and is enshrined at Hōkoku Jinja as Hōkoku Daimyō Jin. When the rule of Hideyoshi's clan ended in 1618, the Tokugawa clan took over and destroyed Fushimi Castle and with it Hōkoku Jinja. It was not until after the Meiji Restoration of 1868 that the shrine was rebuilt in Fushimi. In 1964 it was moved to its current location within the grounds of Ōsaka Castle. At first the shrine had no garden, but in 1972 the Kyōto Garden Association offered to donate a garden to commemorate the Association's fortieth anniversary.[47] Mirei Shigemori was put in charge of the project and presented his design drawing on 3 June 1972. Because the proposed garden was within the precincts of Ōsaka Castle, a registered historical site, both the city and the prefectural governments needed to support

View from elevated platform ❷; gourd-shaped *tsukiyama* in rear ❸

the project in order to get a building permit for the garden from the Agency of Cultural Affairs in Tōkyō. Lobbying and fundraising also took time, but by 12 August the permit was granted. Garden construction finally started on 8 October. The garden was finished by 12 November, and on 13 December an opening ceremony was held. Kyōto Garden Association members had sponsored most of the ¥10 million construction budget.

DESCRIPTION The garden is in shape a large rectangle situated immediately to the east of the shrine building. A large metal gate ➊ marks the entrance at the southwestern corner of the garden, and this leads to an elevated platform ➋ along its southern end. From here is where the garden should be enjoyed.

The scene is dominated by a large gourd-shaped *tsukiyama*[48] made from red-brown concrete ➌.[49] The gourd's mouth is near the southwestern corner of the gravel area, and from there the gourd stretches diagonally to the northeast-

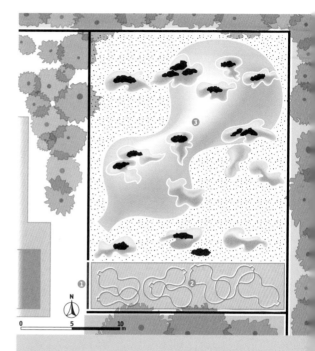

FULL NAME
Hōkoku Jinja Teien, Shūseki-tei (Graceful Stone Garden).

LOCATION ➑ 🗺
Chūō-ku in Ōsaka; the garden is within the castle grounds located in the city center.

CATEGORY
A *karesansui* garden.

THEME
A gourd-shaped *tsukiyama,* a symbolic reference to Toyotomi Hideyoshi, the shrine's patron.

WHEN TO VISIT
The garden is usually not accessible, but a good portion of it can be seen from the gate at any time. Write ahead to the temple for permission to see it or ask about the dates of special events taking place in the garden, such as the outdoor tea ceremony that is sometimes performed on its terrace under a red paper umbrella.

Mouth of gourd: *tsukiyama* in Bengal red-brown concrete

ern part of the garden, covering about 40 percent of its surface. The gourd itself is interlarded by nine smaller gourd-shaped mounds, slightly elevated and covered in moss. Six more similarly shaped islands are spread over the sea of gravel with all but one covered in moss, this being a small concrete island. All together there are fifteen small islands in addition to the large concrete gourd *tsukiyama*.

This scheme of a large gourd with small gourd-shaped islands is then overlaid with a 3-5-7 stone setting. In the south a group of three stones is placed right in front of the viewing platform, with one rock sitting directly in the gravel and no moss surrounding its base. Covering the middle ground is a group of five, all of which sit on a soil mound atop the concrete gourd. The last group of seven contains the tallest stones and occupies the

back of the garden. One stone is on an island to the west of the main gourd. Then immediately east of that island is a triad setting, featuring stones that are 3.2, 2.9, and 2.5 meters tall. Finally, there is a single two-stone group and two single-stone settings.

There are no plants inside the garden except the mix of moss and grass covering the mounds, although many trees along the perimeter have grown so large that some of their branches actually reach into the garden.

The terrace or viewing platform is made from large granite plates, into whose surfaces are

LEFT/RIGHT **Engraved gourd-shapes in surface of elevated platform**

Overview from entrance area with gate to right

carved seven more gourds. The design of the gate is derived from the Chinese characters in "Hōkoku" 豊国, the shrine's name.

The garden was named Shūseki-tei 秀石庭, which is what Mirei Shigemori had proposed. *Shū* 秀 is taken from "Hideyoshi" 秀吉, and *seki* 石 is from "Ishiyama-dera" 石山寺, the name of the temple that had previously existed on the site.

INTERPRETATION As he did quite often in his career, here Mirei Shigemori got to work on a site that had been a place of worship for many centuries. This meant he needed to understand the previous layers of history, but at the same time could

"Nowadays, modern temples and shrine buildings need to be accompanied by modern gardens; we can no longer just keep using the same old rules." [50]

draw inspiration from them. In this case a temple named Ishiyama-dera, literally "Stone Mountain Temple," had existed on this site in ancient times. From this he learned two things: First, there had most likely been a stone mountain or hill here before the first castle was built. And, second, this was usually an indication that there had probably been an *iwakura* here long before that, since after Buddhism came to Japan temples were frequently built on what were already ancient religious sites.

As Shigemori was now faced with the task of designing a garden for a Shintō shrine, he felt it was entirely appropriate to use an *iwakura*-like stone setting to make those old religious roots visible again. Thus his de-

sign refers back to the ancient Shintō belief that *kami* come to visit on particular rocks at certain times of the year. But with the Buddhist trinity stone setting, he incorporates a Buddhist layer into his design as well.[51]

Mouth profile of gourd

Because of the site's proximity to the ocean and Ōsaka's very old harbor, Shigemori also thought it was appropriate to recall an ocean scene here. He explains: "Since ancient times foreign culture entered Japan through these ports, so the notion of the sea was also important for me."[52] This was the motivation to design the garden in *karesansui* style, creating a landscape of islands set within a huge ocean of sand. By design-

ing the biggest island in the shape of a gourd he establishes a link to Toyotomi Hideoshi and thus layers what is historically the site's newest aspect into the garden's design. Remaining true to his principles, Shigemori does this in his own modern way by using concrete and thereby offending all the traditionalists who are convinced that the ancient garden element of the *tsukiyama* can only be made out of soil.

The outcome then not only reflects the power of Toyotomi Hideyoshi's character, as Shigemori would like us believe, but also very much the character of the garden's designer.

LEFT *Tsukiyama* with rocks amid patches of grass   RIGHT View of gate ❶ with design derived from characters of the shrine's name

Fukuchi-in, 1973

High atop Mt. Kōya, Shintō and Buddhism have long coexisted and influenced each other. The garden at Fukuchi-in, which is a Buddhist temple, combines a variety of cultural and religious references in a quite distinctive way. Extensive use of color and form is balanced with vast numbers of clipped azaleas.

HISTORY   In A.D. 816 Kōbō Daishi returned from studying Buddhism in Tang China and was given a piece of property from the emperor. Its isolated location on top of Mt. Kōya seemed the perfect environment for the study and practice of religion. Since it was the emperor, considered the head priest of the nation's Shintō cult, who had bestowed the land, from the outset the emphasis at Mt. Kōya was on the coexistence of the two religions. By the seventeenth century the colony on the mountain had grown to nearly two thousand small huts. After the Meiji Restoration of 1868 the temples there were reorganized, and Kongōbu-ji emerged as the largest among them. The founding date of Fukuchi-in is unknown, but it is today the second-largest temple on Mt. Kōya.

In 1973 Mirei Shigemori was commissioned by the temple's head priest to do a design for the pond garden and the courtyard garden north of the main building. He finished the plan on 27 June and construction began as early as 21 August. By 3 December 1973, the entire back garden was finished. Shigemori must have pleased his clients very much, because within

Aizen-tei ❶, "Garden in the Color of Love," mixes Shintō and Buddhism

a few months he was asked to design the front garden as well. On 1 October 1974 the plan was complete, and by the 15th of the same month construction began. But because of Shigemori's declining health as well as scheduling problems with other projects, everything was put on hold on 16 November, and work on the garden didn't resume until 12 September of the follow-

Grid pattern represents Buddhist solemnity

ing year, resulting in a ten-month break during which the garden remained half finished. Mirei Shigemori had passed away in March 1975, and a team led by his longtime head of construction, Yukio Okamoto, finished the work in accordance with the plans on 4 November 1975.

Stone and gravel grid with azalea *karikomi* as backdrop

DESCRIPTION The garden at Fukuchi-in consists of three main sections: the front garden to the south of the building, a pond, and a courtyard garden in *karesansui* style to the north. As you enter the temple's precincts through the main gate, two paths, one straight and the other curved, lead toward the main building. The straight path draws a diagonal line through the garden and is paralleled by an ornamental fence. The curved path takes you around a group of plants up to the main entrance. Not accessible to visitors is the section behind the bamboo fence, where a straight gravel path leads right up the middle to the temple's *hōjō*, the strong symmetry of the layout emphasizing the importance of that building. A white-and-red grid pattern ❶ covers part of the ground between the path and the main building as well as the area right in front of the *hōjō*. The backdrop to this consists of a series of *tsukiyama* covered in clipped azaleas ❷ and occupied by several stone settings, all of which stretch along the earthen wall on the garden's southern border. The stone settings extend into the gravel plane and continue all the way into the grid, thereby connecting the different features of this section of the garden.

The pond in the back is mostly viewed from the main lobby and contains the usual tortoise-and-crane-island grouping that symbolizes longevity and luck. To the rear a gradual slope is planted with a large *karikomi* ❸ consisting of two types of azaleas. From the west a river flows via a dramatic waterfall into the pond

FULL NAME
Fukuchi-in Teien (Fukuchi-in Garden): Aizen-tei (Color of Love Garden, south garden); Tōsen-tei (Ascending to Paradise Garden, pond garden); Yūsen-tei (Paradise Garden, courtyard garden).

LOCATION ❾ 🗾
Mt. Kōya in Wakayama Prefecture; 80 km south of Ōsaka.

CATEGORY
Two *karesansui* gardens (front garden and courtyard) and one pond garden behind the main building.

THEME
The integration of Shintō and Buddhism, the color of love and paradise.

WHEN TO VISIT
The summit of Kōya-san is 800 meters above sea level and is pleasantly cool in summer, when most of the low-lying parts of Japan are humid and hot. Any time between April and November is great for a visit, with the cherries blooming two weeks later and fall colors starting two weeks earlier than in Ōsaka. If you don't mind snow, winter can be very impressive on Kōya-san with everything white and blanketed.

Shigemori's trademark shape: a series of colorful waves of stone

The ultimate abstraction of the dynamic of nature: scenes of rocks and waves

below. An ornamental water basin makes a quiet accent near the building.

Adjacent to the east is the courtyard garden, surrounded on three sides by buildings and separated from the pond garden by a bamboo fence. It features an imaginary *karesansui* landscape in two colors of gravel with longish mounds of moss. The winding lines give a feeling of a river meandering between mountains ❹.

The garden featured on the front cover of this book is a tiny extension off this courtyard garden to the north side of the main building. In a narrow spot between buildings Shigemori created a spectacular scene of rocks and waves.

"Ponds have been dug and stones have been set in the Japanese garden since ancient times. Natural stones called iwakura *and* iwasaka *were objects of religious belief. In the pond, islands were arranged for the gods. In fact, the original Japanese garden was not made to look at; rather it was made as a sacred place of refuge for the gods."* [53]

Crane island symbolizing luck in front of slope covered in mounds of *karikomi* ❺

Adaptation of form and material: *tsukiyama*

INTERPRETATION An interesting aspect of Japanese temples is that many of the buildings actually started out as residences and were only later converted into temples. Hence the temple garden often had a distinctly residential feel to it, which was even enhanced once guest facilities were added. Fukuchi-in is a good case in point as the line between temple and residential garden is especially vague here.

The front garden presents an interesting juxtaposition of forms and styles, apparently inspired by the history of the place. Mirei Shigemori's son Kanto explains: "The unusual design represents the idea of a mixture of Shintō and Buddhism, as this is what has been practiced on Mt. Kōya since its establishment. So the garden here represents both the solemnity of Buddhism [in the form of the grid] and the ancient *iwakura* of Shintō."[54] The grid marks the front of the building, thereby highlighting the connection between the two. As the temple of Fukuchi-in is dedicated to a god named Aizen Myōō,[55] Shigemori named the front garden Aizen-tei 愛染庭, literally "Garden in the Color of Love," which also explains the red sand, inspired by the color associated with this god. Taoism is represented in the garden in the form of a Hōrai-style stone set-

LEFT/RIGHT **Stone settings refer to Shintō's ancient *iwakura***

ting, a reference to the cult of immortality in ancient Chinese philosophy.[56]

The pond in the back of the main building is an interesting combination of real water with a *karesansui* theme around it: the paving along the shore implies a beach, which is then

TOP / RIGHT **Sand and colored concrete make for an imaginary landscape**

followed by actual sand. The *karikomi* in the back complements the scene well and makes for a dramatic mountain and sea composition, a classic motif executed with a contemporary twist. The garden was named Tōsen-tei 登仙庭, meaning "Ascending to Paradise Garden," a reference to the way the *karikomi* mountains are rising toward the distant background, starting from the ocean and beach near the building. In the back, as well as in the front garden, the mounds of clipped azaleas have another important role: they serve to balance the visual activity created by the various shapes and colors.

The courtyard garden's river landscape could well be inspired by the famous hills around Yangshou that are so often depicted on Japanese scroll paintings.[57] Mirei Shigemori named this garden Yūsen-tei 遊仙庭, which can be translated as "Paradise Garden." For him this was where the human soul would go to play and seek the truth, which is just what the designer himself did before he could finish this work.

Yūsen-tei ❹, "Paradise Garden," with dry river meandering between mountains

Matsuo Taisha, 1975

The garden at Matsuo Taisha is Mirei Shigemori's last work, and its stone setting is considered by many to be one of his very best. With this work he returns to the very roots of the Japanese garden, creating an *iwakura,* a place for the Shintō gods to come and visit.

HISTORY An enormous stone near the top of Mt. Matsuo, just behind Matsuo Taisha, marks the origin of this shrine. This *iwakura* is where the shrine was located in ancient times before it was moved down to its current location in A.D. 701. With the move of the capital to Kyōto in 794 the shrine gained in importance and eventually became one of the Twenty-one Grand Shrines of Japan. The shrine complex's oldest building, the inner shrine, dates back to 1397 and is now designated an Important Cultural Asset. These days the shrine's clientele consists of many miso paste manufacturers and sake brewers, who come here to pray for the success of their businesses.

In October 1973 the new treasure house and a new building for ceremonies were finished, both distinctly modern structures made from concrete. Already in 1971 Mirei Shigemori had been selected as the designer for the adjacent new gardens. The plan was finished on 14 May 1974, and construction started two weeks later on 29 May. Due to the garden designer's declining health the project took almost one year to be completed. The

Jōko no Niwa ❸, "Prehistoric Garden," features one of Shigemori's finest stone settings

Kyokusui no Niwa ❶, "Garden of the Winding Stream," located at the foot of a turtle-shaped mountain

last part of the work was then supervised by his son Kanto after Shigemori passed away on 12 March 1975.

DESCRIPTION The entire Matsuo Taisha project consists of four independent parts, only two of which are covered in this book, the Garden of the Winding Stream and the Prehistoric Garden. The first, called Kyokusui no Niwa 曲水の庭, features a rigorously winding stream ❶ that enters the garden in the southwest corner and leaves it in the north. The banks are covered with flat blue stones and the bottom of the shallow river with gravel. The backdrop is an impressive *karikomi* ❷, a large mound of azaleas roughly in the shape of a turtle, symbolizing the hope for a long life. At the same time it refers to Mt. Matsuo located behind the shrine, which from a distance has a very similar form. Stone settings are spread throughout the garden and make a stark contrast to the smooth *karikomi*. The entire east section of the garden is paved and accessible to visitors who can cross the river via two stone bridges.

The second part of this garden is named Jōko no Niwa 上古の庭, which translates as "Prehistoric Garden," describing the style chosen by the designer and not the time of its construction. Located on a steep slope next to the new treasure house, the garden features a massive stone setting that alludes to the ancient *iwakura*, the origin of not only this particular shrine, but more broadly the Shintō religion as a whole.[58] The farther up the hill the garden goes the more dramatic the stone setting becomes. At the top ❸, rocks weighing five to eight tons are placed at various angles and distances, creating a very powerful movement. Hence the highest point of the *iwakura* is so dynamic that the stones seem poised to fly away at any minute. All of the stones are *aoishi* from Shikoku, Shigemori's absolute favorite for stone arrangements.[59] A low bamboo that is commonly found on rocky mountain ridges covers the ground.

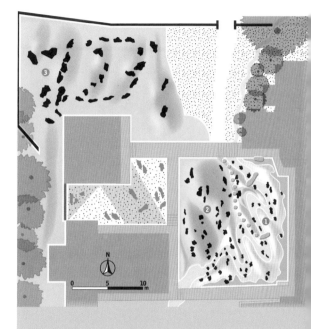

"After the Meiji period, stones were often placed lying down, but this looks weak and lacks vitality. So I decided to go back to the original upright position. Some people find it overwhelming and don't like it. But such people are weak. They lack the power to look at something strong." [60]

INTERPRETATION In few of his gardens did Mirei Shigemori use real water, as he usually pre-

FULL NAME
Matsuo Taisha Teien (Matsuo Taisha Garden): Kyokusui no Niwa (Garden of the Winding Stream); Jōko no Niwa (Prehistoric Garden).

LOCATION ⑩ 🗾
Nishikyō-ku in Kyōto; 7 km west of Kyōto Station.

CATEGORY
A stream and an *iwakura* garden.

THEME
A winding stream at the foot of a turtle-shaped mountain and a powerful stone arrangement as a stopping place for the gods.

WHEN TO VISIT
This is an impressive garden at any time of year and is generally open to the public. The Shinkōsai Festival, dedicated to the temple's god of sake-brewing, takes place on the third or fourth Sunday in April. Its *mikoshi* procession that crosses the river with its participants holding up masks of the deity makes a trip to the garden during festival time very worthwhile.

ferred the abstracted version of the white sand plane. But the little stream coming down Mt. Matsuo just south of the new buildings must have been

About to fly away: dynamic stones at the highest point of the Jōko no Niwa

too tempting to ignore. Shigemori integrated the available water in a *yarimizu* design, a winding-stream element already popular in Heian period (794–1185) gardens. The *karikomi* as a backdrop is also a comparatively infrequent design element among Shigemori's gardens, even though he had used it just two years earlier at Fukuchi-in. These two elements together make for a unique and untypical garden, at least when compared with what Shigemori had created in the past forty-five years.

Unlike Buddhist temples, shrines had long existed in Japan without a designed garden around them. Initially the *iwakura* in its natural setting was worshiped. The rock itself and its surroundings were sometimes cleared of vegetation, and there is some evidence that here and there stones might have been added, but hardly more than that. Around the time that Buddhism came to Japan, Shintō too started to build shrines near or on the sites that had been

Taking the role of the gods: setting stones of the *iwakura* of the Jōko no Niwa

worshiped for centuries. But in contrast to the Buddhist temples, few Shintō shrines ever had anything close to what we would call a garden near their buildings. Shigemori noticed this early on in his career and always remarked that the shrine garden as a style still needs to be created.[61]

Massive *aoishi* from Shikoku are part of the garden's attraction

Yarimizu design: river winding back and forth between the stones   TOP/RIGHT **Banks of stream covered in flat blue stones**

This historical background is what motivated Shigemori to create what he called a Prehistoric Garden at Matsuo Taisha, and it is the *iwakura* behind the current shrine that then inspired his stone setting. In a way he returned to what he saw as the origin of the Japanese garden, especially the *karesansui* garden that so fascinated him, and brought it back into the garden right next to the new buildings of the shrine, thereby making the garden's ancient roots visible again.

According to Shigemori, to place stones as he did here at Matsuo Taisha is to take on the role of the gods: "To set the stones of an *iwakura*, the garden maker should be of the same mentality as the gods, otherwise it can never become a true *iwakura*. But it is impossible to actually become identical to the gods. So what this is all really about is how close a garden maker can get to the gods and how pure his mind can become. That is easy to say but it is very difficult to do."[62] While working on the stone arrangement at Matsuo Taisha, Mirei Shigemori emptied his mind as best as he could and let himself be guided by the voice of the gods. The result is a divine piece of stone-arrangement art.

PREVIOUS SPREAD LEFT *Iwakura:* **a stone arrangement as a stopping place for the gods**   PREVIOUS SPREAD RIGHT **Gravel and light in riverbed**

Afterword

It took a lifetime of experience to be able to envision most of the gardens in this book. In his mid-sixties, when other people are just about to retire, Mirei Shigemori embarked on his most creative period and built some of his best avant-garde gardens. Eight of the ten gardens featured in this book were in fact created in the last fifteen years of his life.

One of the secrets of Mirei Shigemori's success was his ability to persuade his clients. From his point of view that was a design exercise all in itself: "Before the garden maker designs the garden he must thoroughly design the owner. Unless the garden maker can keep the owner in check, the garden design will fail from the beginning. A garden maker who can't design an owner can't design a garden either."[63]

Shigemori obviously had the necessary authority and standing be-fore his clients. In a calm voice he would again and again explain why he was proposing shapes and colors different from the old ones. Furthermore, much of his writing on gardens, some of which his clients naturally had read, focuses on the problem of cultural renewal in a modern age. They could thus see his garden works as a built-manifesto—samples of how Mirei Shigemori thought a contemporary garden should look.

Point and Line to Plane—and Back to Stones

Looking back chronologically on the ten gardens presented in this book, the reader can easily identify how the artist Mirei Shigemori developed. At first, at Tōfuku-ji's main hall, Shigemori seems to be starting his career with a garden full of points. From the square stones dotting the mossy area of the north garden, to the point-like base stones describing the Big Dipper, all the way to the upright stone settings in the south garden pointing straight to the sky, this garden's basic theme could well be the element of the point.

Then toward the middle of the book you can suddenly see lines appearing on the planes of gravel or stone. Of course lines have always been raked into the sand, but the lines that Mirei Shigemori introduces are solid and made from concrete. The line at Sumiyoshi Jinja, for example, becomes an independent design element and is played against the points of black stone and a plane of light gray gravel. It is worth noting that the plane at this time is still one large sea of sand in a single color.

But soon thereafter the line retreats and just marks the edge between two or more fields of differently colored material, be it sand or even concrete. With the design for Sekizō-ji planes of color become the dominant feature in the garden. And at Hōkoku Jinja Shigemori even starts to mound the plane, coming closer to the *tsukiyama*, the old garden element of manmade mounds.

At Fukuchi-in finally he brings back the grid from the very first garden portrayed in this book, though on a different scale and not surprisingly in two colors of gravel.

In Mirei Shigemori's very last work, however, none of the above seems important anymore. With the powerful *iwakura* stone setting at Matsuo Taisha he in fact returns to the very roots of the Japanese garden as he saw them, creating a place for the gods to visit. Obviously he had done many stone settings over his long career as a garden maker, but few if any come up to this last piece. The images in the last chapter of this book speak for themselves.

It seems as if Shigemori had wanted to prove, before leaving this world, that he could very well make great gardens without geometric elements like lines and planes of color, and still remain—as he always put it—eternally modern.

Looking back over Shigemori's career it seems quite obvious how his early education as a painter was at the foundation of his unique approach to the renewal of the Japanese garden. And we can easily imagine how throughout his career as a garden maker Shigemori continued to draw inspiration from his artistic background. Equally important, however, his explorations into the roots of the Japanese garden led him to trace the origin of the ancient craft back to the worshiping of gods, gods who these days still come to visit a very old tree or a fine old stone in a Mirei Shigemori garden.

Mirei Shigemori's greatest contribution to the modernization and renewal of the Japanese garden is without a doubt the moss garden at the *hōjō* of Kyōto's Tōfuku-ji temple. The image of its square stones, scattered over a dark green plane of moss, has literally gone around the world and can be found in every book on the Japanese garden these days. While many were shocked at the time it was made, especially the rather conservative local gardeners, the garden has since then become synonymous with the contemporary Japanese garden and an icon for its modernization. It was an early masterpiece that eventually opened many doors for Mirei Shigemori, and he ended up working on this vision for the rest of his life. With the north garden at Tōfuku-ji he liberated the Japanese garden, which was being held hostage by its own long tradition.

It is interesting, however, that one rarely sees any of Shigemori's other garden designs in Western books on the Japanese garden. Apparently, none of their authors knew about these gardens, meaning that most of Shigemori's rather extraordinary creations have not yet reached the world outside Japan. This fact certainly was a constant surprise while I was researching Shigemori's work.

What Can We Learn from Mirei Shigemori's Work?

Much of Shigemori's work is rooted in traditional Japanese religion and culture. Some Western designers may therefore feel there is nothing they can learn from it. Yet in every culture there are resonant elements from which a designer can create meaningful but modern works. Shigemori produced some great examples of how a specific art, in this case the Japanese garden, can be modernized without losing touch with its history and local environment. In these times of fast globalization a sense of place is increasingly what many new designs are missing. Here Shigemori's very contemporary Japanese gardens, with their distinct connection to the local culture, are a perfect example of how a native sensibility can be modernized without losing its identity to an indifferent global style.

There is already a resurgence of interest in Shigemori's work, from abroad as well as from within Japan. The heirs these days get numerous requests for information, and many people ask to see Shigemori's house and garden in Kyōto. University students are studying his works and write papers about him, while professors cite his books and use his gardens in their lectures and for studio projects. The works of Shigemori seem much less radical in the context of today's Japan than they must have felt at the time of their creation.

Two New Ways of Seeing the Japanese Garden

Most Japanese gardens are designed to be enjoyed with one's eyes, often from a location or path predetermined for the visiting viewer. This usually limits our experience of these places to the visual scenes composed for us. Thus some of these gardens are like a museum where we come to look at a painting hung up for us to appreciate. The real world is a bit more complex and sometimes lacks a frame, so when we visit a Japanese garden we really get to see but a part of its beauty. Markuz's images seem to prove my point. Much of the beautiful texture and detailing that we see through his lens is hardly visible to the ordinary garden visitor.

So this book might actually offer two unusual views of the Japanese garden, the first by portraying the avant-garde garden designs of Mirei Shigemori, and the second by allowing some visual "in-sights" that are usually off limits to the observer.

Colorful, modern, and out of the ordinary: a garden of rock and water at Yūrin no Niwa

Notes

INTRODUCTION

1 "Niwa to Watashi" (Gardens and Me) in *Tampō no Niwa*, listed as Supplement 2 to *Gendai no Niwa* (Contemporary Gardens), Tōkyō: Shōgakkan, 1979.

2 *Nihon Kadō Bijutsu Zenshū* (Complete Works of Japanese Flower Arrangement Art), Kyōto: Nihon Kadō Bijutsu Kenseikai, 1930–32.

3 *Kyōto Bijutsu Taikan: Teienhen* (Art in Kyōto: Garden Edition), Tōkyō: Tōhō Shoin, 1933.

4 *Nihon Teienshi Zukan* (Illustrated Book on the History of the Japanese Garden), Tōkyō: Yūkōsha, 1936–39.

5 "Niwa to Watashi." Meiji period:1868–1912; Taishō: 1912–26; Shōwa: 1926–89.

6 "Shinsakuteiki" in *Shigemori Mirei Sakuhinshū: Niwa—Kamigami e no Apurōchi* (Mirei Shigemori's Collected Works: Gardens—Approach to the Gods), Tōkyō: Seibundō Shinkōsha, 1976.

7 *Gardens of Japan*, Kyōto: Nissha, 1949. This is the only book by Mirei Shigemori published in English.

TŌFUKU-JI

8 The impetus for this was a project for the enhancement of the natural landscape of the Higashiyama area, the hills east of Kyōto where Tōfuku-ji is located. Initiated in 1936 by the Forestry Agency of the national government, the project covered the entire nationally owned thirty-six hills of the Higashiyama area, from Mt. Hiei in the north all the way to Mt. Inari in Fushimi-ku, south of Kyōto .

9 Temples in Japan usually charge a rather large amount of money to provide this kind of service, so this was a quite unusual offer.

10 *Nihon Teien Rekiran Jiten* (Japanese Garden History Dictionary), Tōkyō: Tōkyōdō Shuppan, 1974, p. 418.

11 Hōjō, Hōrai, Eijū, and Koryō are sacred islands recorded in ancient Chinese philosophy and play an important role in the cult of immortality. They represent imaginary islands in the East China Sea that are said to be where the immortals dwell. These islands are often depicted in Japanese gardens.

12 "Niwa to Watashi."

13 *Nihon Teienshi Taikei* (Japanese Garden History Survey), volume 27, Tōkyō: Shakai Shisōsha, 1971–76, p. 121.

14 Katsura Rikyū, built in 1653, and Shugakuin Rikyū, completed in 1659, were both estates for noblemen of the time and already prominently featured the grid motif that is so modern in the eyes of Westerners. Although in both estates the pattern is used indoors on *shōji*, it is an artistic expression of its time and one that Mirei Shigemori well observed. Interesting to note is that neither of these gardens was all that famous at the time.

15 On 7 April 1936 Shigemori wrote an article for the *Japan Times* titled "Rittaiteki Kaiga to

shite no Nihon Teien" (The Japanese Garden as a Three-dimensional Painting); this is noted in the diary of that year.

KISHIWADA-JŌ

16 *Nihon Teien Rekiran Jiten*, pp. 108 and 110.
17 Zhuge Liang, in Japan known as Shokatsu-ryō Kōmei, was a famous Chinese tactician of the second century A.D.; his famous eight-bat-tlecamp formation is a defensive formation, not an offensive one.
18 *Nihon Teienshi Taikei*, p. 35.
19 From 22 to 24 October 1955 an outdoor exhibition of modern art of the Byakutōsha group was held at Kishiwada Castle.
20 "Niwa to Watashi."
21 *Nihon Teienshi Taikei*, p. 35.
22 *Nihon Teien Rekiran Jiten*, p. 108.

ZUIHŌ-IN

23 Sōrin Ōtomo (1530–89) was a Christian *daimyō* (a feudal lord) and in 1550 became the twenty-first generation head of the Ōtomo clan in Bungo, now Ōita Prefecture. He was baptized at the age of forty-eight and named Don Francisco.
24 The Kyōto Garden Association, or Kyōto Rinsen Kyōkai, founded by Mirei Shigemori and others in 1932 to study and protect the her-itage of the Japanese garden, was initially an interdisciplinary and rather progressive study group with many like-minded people.
25 "Niwa to Watashi."
26 *Dokuza yūhō* is a famous expression in a catechism, meaning to sit alone on a great mountain, realizing your own existence. It says that a Zen Buddhist priest can find the great-ness of human existence while sitting alone and meditating.
27 *Nihon Teienshi Taikei*, p. 97.

SUMIYOSHI JINJA

28 The fact that a bell tower was built on the property of the shrine, indicates that Bud-dhism and Shintō were actually peacefully coexisting at the time; it was in fact not until the Meiji Restoration (1868) that they were separated.
29 Mirei Shigemori had sketched the undulat-ing line in his diary on 25 July 1966.
30 "Shinsakuteiki" in *Shigemori Mirei Saku-hinshū: Niwa—Kamigami e no Apurōchi*.
31 He had manifested this already in one of his earliest designs, that of the garden for Kasuga Taisha, deriving the 7-5-3 stone settings from the ancient *iwakura* and its overall organiza-tion from the *shimenawa*, a rope made from rice straw that signifies the place where a *kami* descends to earth.
32 Sumiyoshi is chronologically the third of Shigemori's projects to contain a line or lines. He used a rather thin line to depict the outline of clouds at Kōzen-ji in Kiso-Fukushima, and then more dramatic lines for a cloud design at Tōfuku-ji's Ryōgin-an in Kyōto. This is the first use by Shigemori of lines depicting waves.

YŪRIN NO NIWA

33 *Nihon Teienshi Taikei*, p. 79.
34 Amanohashidate is located on the Tango Peninsula in northern Kyōto Prefecture at the Japan Sea and is considered one of the three most scenic places in Japan. The peninsula is 3.6 km long, less then 189 meters wide, and covered with about 8,000 twisted pine trees. The Japanese name translates into "Bridge to Heaven."
35 A bundle of auspicious strips of dried fish or seaweed. Originally *noshi* referred to a bundle of dried abalone strips, wrapped in red and white paper and attached to gifts to symbol-ize a wish for good luck and lasting happiness. These days a *noshi* is usually just a longish, thin, fan-shaped strip attached to a present.
36 "Niwa to Watashi."

TENRAI-AN

[37] "Shinsakuteiki" in *Shigemori Mirei Saku-hinshū: Niwa—Kamigami e no Apurōchi*.

[38] *Nihon Teienshi Taikei*, p. 154.

[39] An important event in Shigemori's adult life was his meeting with Isamu Noguchi and their resulting cooperation on the UNESCO garden in Paris. On 18 April 1957 Shigemori and Noguchi met for the first time in Himi on the island of Shikoku. Their relationship developed over the course of the UNESCO garden project, and Noguchi remained a frequent visitor to the Shigemori residence thereafter. The Tenrai-an garden was built twelve years later.

[40] *Nihon Teienshi Taikei*, p. 156.

SEKIZŌ-JI

[41] The current name Sekizō-ji is written 石像寺 but had been changed from 石蔵寺, which was read as Iwakura-ji, referring to the *iwakura* up on the hill. The first character 石 means "stone" or "rock" and is usually read as *seki* or as *iwa*. The character 蔵 in the middle of the old name signifies "storage" and can be pronounced *zō* as well as *kura*, like in the word *iwakura*. The Chinese characters used in the old name could thus also be read as Sekizō-ji. Then at one point the middle character was changed to 像, meaning "statue" and read as *zō*, which then excluded the old reading of *kura*; hence, from this point on the temple was called Sekizō-ji, which literally translates as "Rock Statue Temple."

[42] Masao Nonoguchi was also the head of the followers at Sumiyoshi Jinja where Mirei Shigemori built a garden in 1966.

[43] *Shishin sōō* 四神相応 is the name of a concept for a site layout based on the ancient Taoist idea that a land area is protected by the following four gods: *seiryū* 青竜, the Blue Dragon; *byakko* 白虎, the White Tiger; *suzaku* 朱雀, the Red Phoenix; and *genbu* 玄武, the Black Tortoise. This is a geomantic concept, already seen on paintings in ancient tombs, that even-

tually became part of Feng Shui. The layout of the ancient Chinese capital of Xian as well as that of Kyōto is based on this concept.

[44] This concept ties in with ancient Asian astrology, as Gill Hale explains: "Chinese astrologers identified twenty-eight constellations which, when divided into groups of seven, became the Blue Dragon, White Tiger, Black Tortoise and Red Phoenix. Collectively known as the twenty-eight Lunar Mansions and used in conjunction with the 365.25 divisions of the compass, they enabled ancient astronomers to predict eclipses and locate the exact position of the sun in relation to the moon." From Gill Hale, *The Feng Shui Garden*, Singapore: Asiapac Books, 1998, pp. 54–55.

[45] "Shinsakuteiki" in *Shigemori Mirei Saku-hinshū: Niwa—Kamigami e no Apurōchi*.

[46] *Nihon Teienshi Taikei*, p. 45.

HŌKOKU JINJA

[47] The Kyōto Garden Association had already for its thirtieth anniversary donated the garden at Zuihō-in in the Daitoku-ji complex in Kyōto.

[48] Gourds remind every Japanese person of Toyotomi Hideyoshi, who was a leading warrior appointed by the emperor as his shogun in charge of conquering barbarian territories and is to this day remembered as the unifier of Japan. Now what is the connection of this warrior with the gourd? As Hideyoshi rode on a horse with his mounted followers, one of his infantrymen would walk ahead of him, carrying a banner with the seal of the leader. Hideyoshi liked gourds, so he hung a big gourd upside down at the tip of the banner-pole. To this he would add a small gourd every time he won a battle. This cluster came to be called Sennari-byōtan, which literally means "one thousand gourds growing on a tree." It eventually became a symbol for Hideyoshi's great success and remains a powerful sign to this day.

[49] This distinctive color, a reddish brown,

comes from an iron oxide color pigment for concrete called Bengal Indian Red by the manufacturer, the Bayer Corporation of Germany.

50 "Shinsakuteiki" in *Shigemori Mirei Sakuhinshū: Niwa—Kamigami e no Apurōchi.*

51 The Japanese have the great ability to integrate several religions in their everyday lives (and gardens): they grow up with Shintō rituals, marry in Christian chapels, and get buried by a Buddhist priest. What a peaceful place the world would be if more cultures were so tolerant!

52 *Nihon Teienshi Taikei*, p. 94.

FUKUCHI-IN

53 "Niwa to Watashi."

54 Kanto Shigemori in *Nihon Teienshi Taikei*, p. 52.

55 The god Aizen Myōō is originally from India and was later adopted into esoteric Shingon Buddhism.

56 Mt. Hōrai is said to be located in the East China Sea. This legendary sacred island is the home of the immortals and is often depicted in Japanese gardens. In Mirei Shigemori's gardens it is usually depicted by the tallest group of stones. See n. 11.

57 A scenic landscape where the wide Lijiang river meanders between narrow but very tall limestone mountains; located south of Guilin in China's Guangxi Province.

MATSUO TAISHA

58 Shintō —literally, the way of the gods—is the indigenous faith of the Japanese people and is as old as Japan itself. It was originally an amorphous mix of nature worship, fertility cults, divination techniques, hero worship, and shamanism. Today it remains Japan's major religion in addition to Buddhism. Shintō gods are called *kami*. They are sacred spirits that take the form of objects in nature as well as embody concepts important to human life, such as wind, rain, mountains, trees, rivers,

and fertility. Humans become *kami* after they die, at which time they are revered by their families as ancestral *kami*. The *kami* of extraordinary people are even enshrined at some shrines. An altar, the *kamidana* (godshelf), is given a central place in many homes. The Sun Goddess Amaterasu is considered Shintō's most important *kami*.

Shintō is an optimistic faith; humans are thought to be fundamentally good, and evil is believed to be caused by evil spirits. Consequently, the purpose of most Shintō rituals is to keep away evil spirits by purification, prayers, and offerings to the *kami*.

Shintō shrines are the places of worship and the homes of *kami*. Most shrines celebrate festivals (*matsuri*) regularly in order to show the *kami* the outside world. But ancient Shintō did not bother to erect shrines until the third and fourth centuries. The introduction of Buddhism in the sixth century was followed by a few initial conflicts, but the two religions were soon able to coexist harmoniously and even complement each other.

59 For *aoishi*, see the Glossary.

60 From "Niwa to Watashi."

61 Already in 1934 Mirei Shigemori was commissioned to design the Shamusho garden for Kasuga Taisha in Nara, his first large shrine garden project. In volume 22 of *Nihon Teienshi Zukan* he describes the garden and mentions how he struggled to come up with a design that would be related to a Shintō shrine.

62 From *Nihon Teienshi Taikei*, p. 93.

AFTERWORD

63 "Shinsakuteiki" in *Shigemori Mirei Sakuhinshū: Niwa—Kamigami e no Apurōchi.*

Shigemori's Timeline

† Dies at the age of 79 on March 12 in Kyōto — 1975

1971 Starts publishing the updated *Nihon Teienshi Taikei* (Japanese Garden History Survey) in 35 volumes

1964 Publishes *Shigemori Mirei Sakuhinshū: Niwa* (Mirei Shigemori's Collected Works: Gardens), the only book entirely dedicated to his own gardens

1958 Collaboration with photographer Haruzō Ōhashi

1950 Starts *Ikebana Geishitsu* magazine; takes on the role of opinion leader in avant-garde *ikebana* together with Sōfū Teshigahara, Bunpo Nakayama, and Hōun Ohara

First winner of the Kyōto Bunka-in Prize — 1948

1946 Publishes *Nihon no Teien Geijutsu* (Japanese Garden Art) only 1 year after the end of the war

Publishes a total of 33 books between 1940 and 1949

Buys an almost 200-year-old house in Kyōto — 1942

Fourth son Bairon is born on 6 February — 1939

1938 Publishes *Nihon Teienshi Zukan* (Illustrated Book on the History of the Japanese Garden), the result of his survey of some 250 gardens across Japan

September 21 1934 The Muroto Typhoon devastates many gardens in and around Kyōto

1933 Drafts the *Shinkō Ikebana Sengen* (The New Ikebana Declaration) together with Sōfū Teshigahara and Bunpo Nakayama

Third son Geite is born on 19 December — 1935

Daughter Yūgo is born on 15 April — 1930

Moves with his family to Kyōto — 1929

1929 Publishes *Nihon Kadō Bijutsu Zenshū* (The Complete Works of Japanese Flower Arrangement Art)

Second son Koen is born on 27 July — 1926

Changes name from Kazuo to Mirei — 1925

1925 The magazine *Teien* features an article titled "Karesansui and Mister Shigemori's First Work"

Marries Matsue Ochi; First son Kanto is born on 19 May — 1923

Also attends classes at Tōyō University in Indian philosophy; graduates from the Research Dept. of Tōkyō Fine Arts School — 1920

Moves to Tōkyō and enters Tōkyō Fine Arts School to study *nihonga* and continue *ikebana*; becomes interested in philosophy — 1917

Starts taking Fumai-style tea and Ikenobo-style flower-arrangement lessons — 1911

✱ Born in Okayama Prefecture and given the name Kazuo — 1896

BIOGRAPHY

70

1975
1973
1972

⑧ HŌKOKU JINJA

⑦ SEKIZŌ-JI

⑨ FUKUCHI-IN

⑩ MATSUO TAISHA

Starts second survey of all gardens in Japan — 1971

1969

⑤ YŪRIN NO NIWA

⑥ TENRAI-AN

Donates Tenrai-an, his first teahouse, to his hometown of Yoshikawa and creates an avant-garde tea garden around it — 1969

60

1966

④ SUMIYOSHI JINJA

1961

③ ZUIHŌ-IN

茶道

Wife opens the tea-utensil shop Mitsumori in Ōsaka — 1958

Meets Isamu Noguchi and helps him find suitable stones for the UNESCO garden in Paris — 1957

1956 Gardener Yukio Okamoto joins the construction team, building more than 130 projects with Shigemori over the next 19 years

50

1953
1951 Becomes active again as a garden maker in Ōsaka–Kyōto and surrounding areas

② KISHIWADA-JŌ

生け花

Establishes the *ikebana* study group Byakutōsha — 1949

40

1939 Builds the garden at Tōfuku-ji's *hōjō* and 9 more gardens in the Kansai area between 1939 and 1941

① TŌFUKU-JI

書道

Begins first survey of all gardens in Japan — 1936

Helps found Kyōto Rinsen Kyōkai, the Kyōto Garden Association — 1932

Helps found New Ikebana Association — 1930

Works toward a new style of *ikebana* — 1929

30

20

1925 Creates the waterfall stone setting at Tenrai-an, the garden at the family residence, in honor of Dr. Sekino's visit

日本画

Works to establish the University of Culture (Bunka Daigakuin), aiming to take a multidisciplinary approach to Japanese culture — 1922

September 1
1923

The Great Kantō Earthquake interferes with his plans for the University of Culture; moves back to his hometown

1915
1914 Designs his own tearoom Tenrai-an along with his very first garden work

At age 19, designs the *karesansui* garden Sōran-tei for his friend Iga, and creates Gyokuraku-tei garden at his friend Nishitani's house

10

00

ACTIVITIES

Contacts

❶ ⛩ TŌFUKU-JI 東福寺
15-778 Honmachi, Higashiyama-ku
Kyōto 605-0981
〒605-0981京都市東山区本町15丁目778
PHONE: +81 (0)75-561-0087
FAX: +81 (0)75-533-0621
HOURS: 8 a.m. to 4 p.m.

❷ 🏯 KISHIWADA-JŌ 岸和田城
9-1 Kishiki-chō, Kishiwada-shi
Ōsaka 596-0073
〒596-0073 大阪府岸和田市岸城町9-1
PHONE: +81 (0)724-31-3251
FAX: +81 (0)724-31-9706
HOURS: dawn to dusk

❸ ⛩ ZUIHŌ-IN 瑞峯院
Daitokuji-chō, Murasakino, Kita-ku
Kyōto 603-8231
〒603-8231京都市北区紫野大徳寺町
PHONE: +81 (0)75-491-1454
FAX: +81 (0)75-491-1858
HOURS: 8 a.m. to 4 p.m.

❹ ⛩ SUMIYOSHI JINJA 住吉神社
1149 Fukusumi, Sasayama-shi
Hyōgo 669-2513
〒669-2513兵庫県篠山市福住1149
PHONE: +81 (0)79-557-0118
HOURS: by appointment

❺ 🏯 YŪRIN NO NIWA 友琳の庭
1-2 Toyono, Kibichūō-chō
Kaga-gun, Okayama 716-1192
〒716-1192岡山県加賀郡吉備中央町豊野1-2
PHONE: +81 (0)886-54-1313
FAX: +81 (0)866-54-1855
HOURS: dawn to dusk

❻ 🏯 TENRAI-AN 天籟庵
3930-8 Yoshikawa, Kibichūō-chō
Kaga-gun, Okayama 716-1241
〒716-1241 岡山県加賀郡吉備中央町吉川
3930-8
PHONE: +81 (0)866-56-7020
HOURS: by appointment

❼ ⛩ SEKIZŌ-JI 石像寺
1003-1 Nakatakeda, Ichijima-chō
Hikami-gun, Hyōgo 669-4302
〒669-4302兵庫県氷上郡市島町中竹田1003-1
PHONE: +81 (0)79-586-0153
HOURS: dawn to dusk

❽ ⛩ HŌKOKU JINJA 豊国神社
2-1 Ōsaka-jō, Chūō-ku
Ōsaka 540-0002
〒540-0002大阪市中央区大阪城 2-1
PHONE: +81 (0)6-6941-0229
FAX: +81 (0)6-6941-0220
HOURS: the garden can be viewed from the
gate, but entry is by special permission only

❾ ⛩ FUKUCHI-IN 福智院
657 Kōya-san, Kōya-chō, Ito-gun
Wakayama 648-0211
〒648-0211和歌山県伊都郡高野町高野山657
PHONE: +81 (0)736-56-2021
FAX: +81 (0)736-56-4736
HOURS: by appointment
NOTE: this is a Japanese inn and temple

❿ ⛩ MATSUO TAISHA 松尾大社
3 Miyamachi, Arashiyama, Nishikyō-ku
Kyōto 616-0024
〒616-0024京都市西京区嵐山宮町3
PHONE: +81 (0)75-871-5016
FAX: +81 (0)75-871-3434
HOURS: 9 a.m. to 4 p.m.

Locations

JAPAN

0 _____ 500 mls
0 _____ 500 km

RUSSIA
CHINA
SAKHALIN
NORTH KOREA
SOUTH KOREA
Sea of Japan
Sapporo
Hokkaidō
Honshū
North Pacific
Kyōto
Tōkyō
Fukuoka
Kyūshū

GREATER KANSAI AREA

0 _____ 50 mls
0 _____ 50 km

Sea of Japan

Pacific Ocean

Tottori
Maizuru
Kyōto-fu
Gifu-ken
Tottori-ken
Hyōgo-ken
Biwa-ko
Okayama-ken
Sekizō-ji ❼
Zuihō-in ❸
Sumiyoshi Jinja ❹
Shiga-ken
Kyōto
Matsuo Taisha ❿ ❷ **Tōfuku-ji**
Yūrin no Niwa ❺
Tenrai-an ❻
Himeji
Ōsaka
Tsu
Kōbe ❽ **Hōkoku Jinja**
Mie-ken
Setonaikai
❶ **Kishiwada-jō**
Awaji Shima
Nara-ken
Kagawa-ken
SHIKOKU
Wakayama
❾ **Fukuchi-in**
KŌYASAN
Tokushima-ken
Wakayama-ken

Pacific Ocean

CITY OF KYŌTO

0 _____ 1 ml
0 _____ 1 km

KITA-KU
KITAYAMA-dōri
SAKYŌ-KU
UKYŌ-KU
Zuihō-in ❸ 卍
Kitaōji-dōri
Daitokuji Temple District
Horikawa-dōri
KAMIGYŌ-KU
Shirakawa-dōri
Imadegawa-dōri
Imperial Palace
Senbon-dōri
Karasuma-dōri
Kawabata-dōri
Marutamachi-dōri
ASHIYAMA
Nishiōji-dōri
Oike-dōri
Higashiōji-dōri
Sanjō-dōri
Nijō-jō Castle
Shijō-dōri
Gojō-dōri
SHIMOGYŌ-KU
HIGASHIYAMA-KU
❿ 🈲
Matsuo Taisha
Shichijō-dōri
SHIKYŌ-KU
Kyōto Stn.
Kujō-dōri
Tōfuku-ji
❷ 卍
Jūjō-dōri
MINAMI-KU
FUSHIMI-KU

N

❶ Location
卍 Temple
🈲 Shrine
🖾 Public garden
■ City
⋯⋯ Train line
— Street

Glossary

aoishi 青石 a general term for the blue-green stones that are usually used in the Japanese garden. In most cases *aoishi* stones are green schist. Depending on their area of production they are called Kishū Aoishi, Awa Aoishi, Iyo Aoishi, etc. *Aoishi* is a metamorphic rock and naturally occurs in a vein from Tōkyō to Wakayama, Shikoku, and on to Kyūshū. It takes on a variety of shapes and can be found in inland valleys as well as near the ocean.

hōjō 方丈 the main hall or building at a temple complex.

iwakura 磐座 a shrine rock; often a large natural stone outcropping onto which early Japanese believed a god would descend to earth. Revered since ancient times as prayer sites, *iwakura* exist throughout Japan and are thought to contain a *kami* at certain times of the year, or to be a link to the world of the gods. The *iwakura* is also thought to be the origin of stone arranging in Japanese gardens.

kami 神 god(s), of which there are about eight million in Shintō. See also n. 58.

karesansui 枯山水 dry landscape (garden), dry garden; a garden style that probably appeared first in the Muromachi period (1336–1573) and that is unique to Japan. Using neither ponds nor streams, it makes symbolic representations of natural landscapes with stone arrangements, white sand, moss, and pruned vegetation. The term is mentioned already in the ancient garden manual *Sakuteiki*, where it indicates a stone arrangement in a section of the garden without water.

karikomi 刈込み trees and shrubs shaped by trimming; often found in dry landscape gardens of the mid-Muromachi period. Sometimes *karikomi* are similar to Western topiary, but generally they are used for more abstract forms.

Sakuteiki 作庭記 "The Book of Gardening," the oldest textbook on the secrets of gardening in Japan. There is no established theory on its authorship or time of compilation. It is generally said that Tachibana no Toshitsuna (1028–94), third son of Fujiwara no Yorimichi, compiled it from his rich experience seeing and hearing many things about Shinden, or palace-style, gardening from childhood and from his keen observations of nature.

shakkei 借景 borrowed scenery, a technique in which landscape outside the garden is used not as a mere backdrop but as an essential element of its design.

shōji 障子 a paper sliding door. This traditional screen or window covering consists of a wooden lattice and semi-opaque panels of white or slightly textured Japanese paper.

tsukiyama 築山 an artificial earthen hill in the garden. In actual size a *tsukiyama* can be anything from a 1-meter mound to a small hill; small hills are created with soil, and larger hills with rock infill.

tsukubai 蹲踞 the washing facility typically found in a tea garden, consisting of a washbasin (usually made of stone) and a group of keystones.